The Atheist and The Afterlife – An Autobiography

A true story of inspiration, transformation, and the pursuit of enlightenment

By

Ray Catania

Printed in the United States of America
ISBN (paperback) 978-0-578-83257-9
ISBN (ebook): 978-0-578-83184-8

Summation

What would happen if an atheist visited the afterlife?

Once an atheist, now a clairvoyant medium. Follow one man's extreme transformation in this multifaceted memoir, which brings you through a life filled with trauma, death, denial, personal development, paranormal experiences, mediumship, spiritual gifts, true love, and triumph in his ultimate search for enlightenment.

Based on real-life accounts of the author.

Acknowledgements

Honored and grateful to everyone who has ever touched my life, without whom this book would not have been written.

Content Warning

This book deals with adult subject matter and uses adult language that may not be suitable for all readers. Possible triggers include assault, abuse, sex, sexual assault, suicide, violence, profanity, PTSD, near-death experiences, and death.

Categories

Non-Fiction – Autobiographical – Metaphysics – Parapsychology – Personal Development – Psychic Ability – Paranormal Activity – Enlightenment – Spirituality – Inspirational – Memoir

Contents

Dedication

For My Love

Preface

What you are about to read is my life story. A story of how I began this life without any beliefs in any higher power. It's a transformation of over forty years in the making. The book has three parts, with the first being about my life. You'll need to understand where I came from in order to appreciate where I am now. Most people who start out the way I did might wind up in jail or dead, and trust me, there are parts of the book that will make you wonder how I circumvented that destiny as well. This book however, is a major part of that transformation and describes what or who helped me and why.

The second part of the book will take you through the love story between Jessica and me. Jessica opened my eyes to the things that were happening around me that I simply took for granted. I had never thought of myself as special or gifted, but she saw it, and she pushed me to learn about my differences and find out how to evolve. Meeting Jessica was no coincidence. In fact, if there is one thing that I learned from Jessica, it is that there are no coincidences in life.

The third part of this book examines the science attributed to my theories of these abilities. I do not believe in anything unless it can be proven scientifically. The science is based on my studies of the research by the many great physicists, astronomers, and scientists of our time. The most prevalent for me and this book include Tesla, Einstein, Dirac, Bohr, Schrodinger, and Heisenberg. I should also mention the late, great astronaut, Edgar Mitchel, whose teachings, drive, and determination for there to be more scientific research done on this topic inspired me as well.

A few things about me. I dislike the term psychic, as do most psychics, I think. The term psychic has become synonymous with fraudulent behaviors. I am nothing more than a human being with a partially enlightened consciousness or intuitive/medium, if such a label is required. One can achieve many levels of enlightenment; I have barely scratched the surface, and I've only just begun to climb the tall mountain that is enlightenment. I have much to learn and a long way to go.

This story will take you through the journey of my realization and process over time. I can see some things, hear some things, feel some things, and know some things that others cannot pick up on. I do not see, hear, or feel with my natural senses. If I did, I would likely be considered schizophrenic or to have some other type of mental illness. Pictures, thoughts, and feelings enter my mind, and although I may refer to them as sights, sounds, and feelings, that is because I have no other way to explain these phenomena in terms that most people would understand.

I am not a self-proclaimed expert on the subject matter at hand. I wrote this book as I was learning and experiencing these events for myself the first time around, so you will find that I explain things in layman's terms. There are certain phenomena mentioned within this story that have already been given proper names by the psychic community and are being explored by other folks who have been doing this a lot longer than I. You'll notice, therefore, that at times I make up names for the phenomena I was unable to explain when they first occurred. Later in my learning process, I went back and updated some of these to their proper names as they are referred to in the psychic world today.

I am in the process of learning how to make this happen when I want it to happen and not just whenever "it" feels like happening or coming to me. That is my challenge. The two teachers I currently work with have helped many law enforcement agencies solve crimes, find missing persons, and prevent terrorism. They have somewhat mastered their abilities, and I would like to do the same. The point of this book is two-fold: the first is that, if I can do this, anyone can do this, and the second is that these incredible events may be happening around you already and you're not noticing them, so I hope to bring awareness of them to you.

Throughout this book, I speak of these experiences in a lighthearted and sometimes sarcastic tone, and I use a lot of profanity, so I am not what you may be used to in a "spiritual" person. I hope not to offend anyone, but I see a lot of humor in this. Life doesn't have to be serious all the time.

When you finish reading all three parts, I hope to leave you with a sense of peace and calm knowing that there is so much more to our conscious mind and its journey. The body that your consciousness lies within is but one step on a great pathway to much more after the body is gone. I hope you will find peace in knowing that death brings more pain to the living than the deceased. Our loved ones are not gone; they have just transformed.

I was an atheist. I stepped into the afterlife, and I returned. This is the story of my journey through this life and my ongoing search for the ultimate enlightenment. I hope you enjoy it. Perhaps you'll relate to it in more ways than you think.

Thank you.

Introduction

I would like you to know the definitions of the following terminology and how it specifically relates to my writings.

Please do not assume you understand the meanings below as they are going to be used in this book. It is quite important to understand what my definitions of these terms are and, more importantly, to understand what they are *not* before you continue reading this book. (Cited sources are noted respectively, where necessary.)

Parapsychology: "The study of mental phenomena which are excluded from or inexplicable by orthodox scientific psychology. Parapsychology is the scientific and scholarly study of three kinds of unusual events. Extrasensory perception, mind-matter interaction, and survival, which are associated with human experience. The existence of these phenomena suggests that the strict subjective/objective dichotomy proposed by the old paradigm may not be quite as clear-cut as once thought. Instead, these phenomena may be part of a spectrum of what is possible, with some events and experiences occasionally falling between purely subjective and purely objective. We call such phenomena 'anomalous' because they are difficult to explain within current scientific models."—PBS.Org

What is not Parapsychology: "In spite of what the media often imply, parapsychology is not the study of anything Paranormal or bizarre. Nor is Parapsychology concerned with astrology, UFOs, searching for Bigfoot, the Loch Ness monster, paganism, Satanism, vampires, alchemy, or witchcraft."—PBS.Org

Metaphysical: Derived from the Greek *meta ta physika* ('after the things of nature'), metaphysical refers to an idea, doctrine, or posited reality outside of human sense perception. In modern philosophical terminology, metaphysics refers to the study of what cannot be reached through objective studies of material reality.

1

"Metaphysics is a type of philosophy or study that uses broad concepts to help define reality and our understanding of it. Metaphysical studies generally seek to explain inherent or universal elements of reality that are not easily discovered or experienced in our everyday lives. As such, it is concerned with explaining the features of reality that exist beyond the physical world and our immediate senses. Metaphysics, therefore, uses logic based on the meaning of human terms, rather than on a logic tied to human sense perception of the objective world."—PBS.Org

Psychic: "A person who uses extrasensory perception (ESP) to identify information hidden from the normal senses, particularly involving telepathy or clairvoyance, or who performs acts that are inexplicable by natural laws."—Wikipedia.Org

You must be psychic to be a medium, but you need not be a medium to be psychic. They have different abilities.

Clairvoyance: "Derived from French *clair* meaning 'clear' and *voyance* meaning 'vision,' [clairvoyance] is the ability to gain information about an object, person, location, or physical event through extrasensory perception."—Wikipedia.Org

Mediumship: "The practice of purportedly mediating communication between spirits of the dead and living human beings. Practitioners are known as 'mediums' or 'spirit mediums'."—Wikipedia.Org

Dimension: "A dimension is technically a pair of opposite directions: Length is the first dimension, width is the second, height is the third. (Ignore 'time' for now; while 'time' is dimension-like in some ways, it works differently in practice.) Now imagine a fourth spatial dimension perpendicular to the other three. By traveling along that dimension, one might wind up in another 3-D space. So, you're not really traveling to 'another dimension'; you are traveling through another dimension (direction) to reach an inaccessible place. Some fiction writers often use 'another dimension' to mean 'another universe.' This is the wrong way to use this word."—Worldbuilding.stackexchange.com

Realm: This literally means "a kingdom," where each region of existence is ruled over by its own cosmic entity or energy being. Some might use "dimension" or "plane" for this purpose, but technically it isn't an accurate use of those words. It is just what other literary agents have done.

For the purpose of this book, I have chosen this definition.

"A Realm is another place in the Universe where there are energy beings that are separated from other energy beings, either by their knowledge, status, ability, physical state of being, or plane. They may or may not also be separated physically and therefore making them physically unable to enter another Realm."—Worldbuilding.stackexchange.com

Mindfulness: "A mental state achieved by focusing one's awareness on the present moment, while calmly acknowledging and accepting one's feelings, thoughts, and bodily sensations, used often as a therapeutic technique."—Dictionary.com

Energy Beings: This refers to a consciousness living outside the physical body. Some may refer to it as a spirit or soul; however, I choose to avoid these terms whenever possible, as there are too many preconceived notions about them.

Guides: These are energy beings living in a higher realm of reality with tremendous insight, intelligence, and who will typically offer guidance and support to someone or something. To me, they present themselves in singular form or a panel of three or seven.

It is important to note that some mediums believe that guides and masters are actually deceased folks who you have known or who know you and wish to help you, but they choose not to reveal their identity to you. They are not necessarily assigned to you to help you, but we know they exist. They do not appear in human form.

Masters: Energy beings at a much higher level of reality with incredible force, power, insight, and intellect. They typically present themselves in a panel of seven or eleven.

The Divine Being(s): All-powerful, all-knowing, energy being, of or in the highest known realm of reality and consciousness. I only know of one thus far.

He/Him: A pronoun used throughout this book to refer to beings where a sexual orientation cannot be confirmed or identified.

First Law of Thermodynamics: "Also known as the Law of Conservation of Energy, states that energy can neither be created nor destroyed; energy can only be transferred or changed from one form to another."—Wikipedia.Org

Dark Energy: "The force that is believed to be making the universe larger. Distant galaxies appear to be moving away from us at high speed. The idea is that the universe is getting bigger and has been since the Big Bang due to this unidentifiable energy force."—Wikipedia.Org

Dark Matter: "Matter composed of particles that do not absorb, reflect, or emit light, so they cannot be detected by observing electromagnetic radiation. Dark matter is material that cannot be seen directly. We know that dark matter exists in our universe because of the effect it has on objects that we can observe directly."—Wikipedia.Org

From the author:

If you are anything like I was—a complete sceptic of all things related to the subject of parapsychology—then I have a suggestion for you. Below is a list of documentaries that I have watched, each of which contains some important information and concepts that I have used to address and explain the science in this book. For me to believe, I had to have these facts placed in front of me. This won't cover every aspect of the science in this book, but it is a good place to start. I realize that no matter what scientific research I present, some folks may never open their minds to the possibilities of these concepts, and while that is unfortunate, I completely respect their choice. In no way, shape, or form will

I ever try to change anyone's beliefs. Nor will I try to persuade anyone into agreement.

1. ***Einstein's Quantum Riddle***, released by Nova Productions in January 2019, is a documentary that explains the scientific theory of how one sub-atomic particle can alter or affect another sub-atomic particle simultaneously regardless of distance, space, or time. The two sub-atomic particles can be right next to each other or in different galaxies and nonetheless react to one another at the exact same time. All sub-atomic particles must therefore contain and transfer energy. Albert Einstein eventually had to concede to physicist Niels Bohr's correct understanding of the atomic structure and his "Quantum Theory." Bohr's discovery was the beginning of what we now call Quantum Mechanics. This idea was originally rejected by Einstein when he referred to this concept as "a spooky action at a distance."

2. ***Everything and Nothing***, released by Furnace Productions and the BBC in March 2011, is a documentary explaining scientifically how scientists discovered that there is no such thing as nothing. Even in the vacuum or void of space, there is always "something" present. These can be described as quantum fluctuations. To have quantum fluctuations, there must be small packets of energy that can appear and disappear in the vacuum or void. This suggests that "something" can come from "nothing," and it likely occurs due to "dark" energy, which we cannot see. The vacuum, the void, or what appears to be empty space is actually alive with energy. These findings are based on Quantum Mechanics and Werner Heisenberg's Uncertainty Principle. These principles are fundamental to our universe at the sub-atomic level.

3. ***Teslafy Me***, released by Vision Films in 2019, is a documentary based on the discoveries and life of Nikola Tesla. Because Tesla died somewhat in poverty, he seems to be missing from most of

our history books, but if you know anything about him, you know then that the reason he wasn't wealthy is that he wanted to give away his inventions for free, including the transference of electricity. Tesla was working on a way to provide the world with free electricity that would have been generated without burning any fossil fuel and without using any source other than the Earth's natural magnetic field, which is part of our atmosphere. His funding was cut off by J.P. Morgan when Morgan found out Tesla's intentions were to create something that could not be monetized. But that is not why I want you to watch this documentary. Tesla had abilities. His inventions came to him in pictures in his mind, not like traditional inventors such as Thomas Edison, or anyone else for that matter. Tesla also understood that information could be transmitted through the Earth's electromagnetic field, just like electricity. He envisioned the mobile phone and all of its capabilities around 1900. He called it an information transferring device, and he predicted that it would one day fit in your pocket. He was, by all accounts, a clairvoyant who was receiving information that was far ahead of his time. His famous quote, "If you want to understand the secrets of the universe, think in terms of energy, frequency, and vibration." Tesla went as far as to not shake hands with others so as not to alter his energy by touching someone else's. He refused to get married, so he would not be obligated to interact with another person regularly who may alter his state of energy and consciousness, especially if he was working on something important. He recognized what we now call the "collective consciousness" and how we all affect one another with our individual energy, frequency, and vibration.

4. *5ᵗʰ Dimension* **(Season 1 Episode 6)—"Telepathy,"** released by Parthenon Entertainment in 2006, is a documentary about the uses of telepathy during the Cold War between Russia and the United States. Both countries were exploring the possibilities of what could be done if they, or the other side, had people with

these abilities. "Psy Agents," short for Psychic Agents, refers to the agents who worked for the military for well over twenty years. Interviewed for this film is one of the men who helped the USA for many of those years. His superior officers were also interviewed in this documentary. The Psy Agents were tasked with remote viewing (of the enemy), which is a form of ESP where one can "see" in their mind's eye, other people, places, or things anywhere in the world. They can be given very little information to perform this task. This documentary should leave you with little doubt that some people have their sixth sense, as is it called, fully developed. What I found quite interesting about this film and the other folks who I personally know that have their sixth sense fully developed is that one common denominator made it all begin: trauma. Repeated exposure to trauma often combined with near-death experiences.

The second documentary on the list, entitled *Everything and Nothing*, is part of a complete series called *Quark Science* that, if you have the time to invest in watching them all, are simply mind-blowing and so well produced for those who enjoy science. I could add so many books and documentaries to this list, but that would be a book in itself, so I have narrowed it down to the ones that make the point quickly and efficiently.

Part I
The Experience—"My Life"

CHAPTER 1:

Let's Go Yankees!

Today, I am sitting just a few rows away from the third baseman for the New York Yankees at Yankee Stadium as they play in the 2019 American League Championship Series. It is the fourth game of the best of seven series, and it is a must-win for the Yankees, who are losing the series two games to one. There is a small handful of people between me and the field. The price of these tickets could probably feed a small, hungry city for one day. I typically don't spend money frivolously because I never had any growing up. I have too much respect for money to give it away unless I am actually feeding the poor, but this was something I had to do for myself. Plus, my girlfriend is a huge Yankee fan, and I knew she would love these seats, but actually, there is something much greater than a baseball game happening on this day for me. Something beautiful.

I had a moment during the national anthem when a tear ran down my face. On the verge of getting emotional, I quickly refrained because I was embarrassed. Truth be told, I was so grateful to be here. I was so grateful that I am now in such a good place in life with my career, my self-made money, a loving girlfriend by my side, and two amazing children, who I make certain always have it better in childhood than I ever did.

I am the kind of dad who listens, communicates calmly and rationally, and does not use alcohol or drugs to cloud my judgment. I treat my children with respect. I hug them and tell them how much I love them every day, just in case it is my last day on Earth. I was the first to change their diapers. I went to parent teacher conferences, took them to practice, and ran a company. I was and I still am Super Dad! This is because being someone's dad is my reason for living.

It was forty-four years ago when I dreamed of playing for the New York Yankees. I would hide out in my small bedroom at home, locking the door as a seven-year-old boy with a baseball in my hand and the radio nearby to listen to each and every Yankee game played. The Yankees were always on the radio, and they played so many games that I always had some form of entertainment. We didn't have cable television or personal computers. They weren't invented yet. This was the 1970s when the NY Yankees were the most dominant team in all of baseball. They never let me down.

Sometimes, I would take the radio and the ball and hide in a closet or in the yard or in the basement of my parents' home. I was alone, but I was okay with that because I needed to stay clear of what was happening in my home: fighting, yelling, and loved ones saying the most hurtful things to each other. Doors slamming, things breaking, and—well, you get the idea.

Just me, the radio, and a baseball, and I was a seven-year-old New York Yankee superstar—in my mind anyway. We didn't have much in those days. We were okay, but we could barely afford to live in our middle-class community. We were always struggling for money. We struggled to get through the day and then at nightfall, all hell broke loose and I certainly wanted nothing to do with that.

I figured if I could stay hidden until it was over, I would be spared being a part of this daily fighting ritual. Sometimes it worked and other times it did not, but in my mind, being alone and hidden away from the rest of the world, I could be anyone I wanted to be or have anything I wanted. I really wanted a friend, but since I was alone, I would just make them up. I would communicate with them in my mind.

I had a slightly younger brother whom I loved very much—and I still do, of course—but I doubt he knew that back then because, at that time in my life, I didn't know how to express love without my anger being attached to it. Therefore, he and I would just end up fighting. So, I ended up isolating myself and began to communicate instead with my "imaginary friends"—and one day they answered me. It was in my mind, so I was not hearing voices, but I was communicating with someone or something that wasn't visible. As a child, this did not scare me one bit. I was thrilled, and as time went on, I made more friends this way. I had no preconceived notions that this wasn't real or all in my head. I just went with it. They were my friends. They guided me through some really bad times. I am eternally grateful for them.

I once revealed that I had these friends to one of my living friends. She was okay with my imaginary friends, but later revealed my secret to her parents, who then told my parents. I was completely humiliated, and I never spoke to my so-called imaginary friends again, but they were always there. They would change over the years. Some "friends" would leave and other new ones would arrive during my youth, but I continually told myself that they weren't real: "It's all in your head. Let it go." I would never mention them again, and I didn't communicate with them any longer. But, when I was in trouble or about to be in trouble, a voice would return and tell me immediately what to do to get the hell out of there and save myself, always at the last possible second. I learned to just take the advice, as it was always the correct thing to do.

I had the Catholic religion essentially forced upon me, and I wasn't allowed to dispute anything the Bible said. However, even as a very young boy, I pointed out that the ten commandments were repetitive and sexist. If there was a loving God, why did he like men better than women? A man can't carry a baby to term and deliver it into the world. It sure seemed to me that women could do things men couldn't. But what did I know? I was just a kid.

I also wondered why children were going hungry in some parts of the world while we were being thankful for our Thanksgiving Day dinner? Did God like some people better than others? Did he like Americans more? It just didn't make sense to me. As I aged, I became agnostic and then eventually atheist, but I would never let on that I had felt this way to anyone in my life, as I'm sure I would have been chastised for having those thoughts.

I have forgiven those who contributed to my tumultuous childhood and have made my peace with it, but it wouldn't be until a decade or more later that I would have another paranormal encounter so profound that there was simply no denying that I had certain abilities that others did not. So how did I handle that? I suppressed it, of course. I denied it repeatedly, like everything else that happened to me. I rationalized that it was something that could happen to anyone. I am referring to my first near-death experience.

It wouldn't be until much later in my adult life that I would concede that I was different and that I had to do something with this ability. I can only imagine what my life would be like had I embraced this sooner.

I am addressing this book to all those people who hurt me the most. The ones who betrayed me. The ones who took advantage of me as a young person. The bullies and the abusers. For without you, I wouldn't be the strongest human being I know today. I wouldn't have been able to inspire others to reach new heights and accomplish their goals. I wouldn't have had enough anger inside me to drive me to success without fear, and I wouldn't be the best dad in the world. At least according to my kids.

CHAPTER 2:
I Think, Therefore I Am

You must know a few things about me before we go any further. For the majority of my life, I have been agnostic, and for part of it, an atheist. I've never believed in astrology, fortune telling, tarot cards, or anything like that. If you cannot prove something to me scientifically, I will not believe it at all. I have never had blind faith in anyone or anything. I trusted almost no one, other than myself.

I have an extremely positive, analytical mind that requires absolute proof of all things. I find the good in even the worst things that life can throw at me or anyone. I have a mathematical mind, and I am successful in business. I do my best to remove any and all emotion from my decision-making process. I am aware that most everyone has an agenda and is self-serving by default, even if they don't mean to be. I believe in Karma, very much so. I believe in the philosophy "do unto others as you'd have them do unto you" as words of law.

I am not self-described as a "people person" or an "animal lover." I respect all living things but do not feel a need for them around me. It's more of a desire to find the select few right ones to have in my life. Quality over quantity, I suppose. I've kept my circle of people small and tight, and it takes a lot for me to let a new person in. I have always been willing to cast someone out of my life in an instant for any type of betrayal, even for just lying to me once.

I have always had a rough, cold exterior that most people find intimidating right off the bat, but if you get to know me, you'll see I am not actually angry all the time. It's more my default facial expression. I am, however, hyper-vigilant and always looking over my shoulder, meaning I am ready for bad shit to come my way before it comes my way. I have had a challenging life. My youth was filled with turmoil and emotional abuse, and we were handicapped monetarily. Absolutely nothing was ever given to me. I had to go out and get all that I have and all that I am.

As a result of this set of circumstances, I became an easily angered person. I would never think twice about destroying a person, place, or thing that threatened me or my loved ones. After many experiences where others came at me with their destructive behavior, it just became second nature for me to practice self-preservation and self-defense.

I am an alpha male. I can travel alone or with a small pack of my choosing. My view of others has always been that they are either with me or against me. If you are with me, I will die for you. If you are against me, I will let you die. I am eternally grateful for the loved ones I have and for being able to accomplish the things I have. I never take anyone or anything for granted because I know it can all be taken away in an instant if I don't protect it and show gratitude for it.

I have nearly died several times: I have been shot at; I was nearly blown up by terrorists; I was abused by people I trusted both physically and emotionally as a young man; I died in a fire and was resuscitated; I was in a car crash where I had to be cut free by the jaws of life and another involving a head-on collision with a bus; and I've had at least one incident of alcohol self-poisoning that I can remember. The most amazing thing of all is that physically, I am fine. In fact, I am better than just fine. I am in great health. It was almost as if something was there to scoop me up at the last minute each and every time my life was in danger and showed me how to get through each of these incidents. I'll never understand who or what did that for me. Someone or something not of this Earth had my back time and time again. These events transpired throughout most of my life until I accepted them as a reality.

Needless to say, it took many years of psychological analysis, therapy, and soul searching to begin my personal transformation from who I was then to who I am now, but there were some other things that began to happen in my life during that transition that I could not explain or understand. I am referring to paranormal activity. The metaphysical world just seemed to drop itself on my lap at the most ironic times of my life. This is a significant part of what changed me from the person I was then to the person I am now.

When these strange occurrences began, I thought I was losing my mind. I started to doubt my sanity. I sought the help of doctors, psychologists, psychiatrists, an energy healer, and eventually a medium. Can you guess which ones helped me the most?

Correct! It was when I eventually went to seek help from a well-known evidential medium. One who had worked with the FBI. Anyone who knows me would tell you that I am the last person on the face of the Earth they would ever expect to seek the help of an energy healer or a clairvoyant medium. This is something I would previously have told you was a crock of shit. I was literally the biggest critic of people who said they had a sixth sense. I often defended my position by explaining what a cold reading is or Neuro Linguistic Programing (NLP) and the like. I would explain how a person could get manipulated by a so-called psychic. I was adamant about it; I was certain this was impossible.

I did believe, however, that we all have a certain intuition that some of us can use or tap into better than others. I had often used my "gut feeling" in business and in personal relationships with much success. But psychic? No way! I wasn't buying into that. The actual ability to communicate with things not of this world that we can't see, feel, touch, smell, or hear? Not me! Not yet, anyway.

So why, you ask? Why would a lifetime nonbeliever, agnostic, and atheist choose to consult with an energy healer, clairvoyant, or medium after seeing all the other science-based professionals? Well, this is where my story gets interesting. But, before we go there, you should know a few more things about my childhood.

CHAPTER 3:

The Crayon Incident

The crayon incident occurred when I was in the fourth grade. It was a very disturbing incident, but it will probably give you some insight into who I was as a child. I sat directly across from another student who I considered to be my best friend at the time. The entire class had an arts and crafts project to complete that day. He and I were both working diligently on our individual projects trying to get them done before time ran out.

We each took out our crayons and dumped them on the desks, which were pushed up against one another. As we continued to do our work, coloring our respective projects, my friend noticed he didn't have a blue crayon. His project needed some parts to be colored in blue, and mine also required some blue. So, every time he needed to color something in blue, he would reach over and take my blue crayon without asking. Each time I went to use it, he seemed to have it, so I told him to stop taking my blue crayon. He ignored my request, and I started to get upset about it.

When he repeatedly took my crayon, I got increasingly forceful with my voice, demanding that he stop taking my stuff. He, however, decided not to heed my warnings and continued to do what he wanted.

I got angry that he was completely ignoring me and taking my stuff as he pleased, so I got up and walked away, taking my pencil to the only pencil sharpener in the room. As I sharpened my pencil, I was brewing with anger over the blatant disrespect for me and my stuff. I thought of an idea; I knew what I was going to do.

I returned to the two adjoining desks and sat staring at that blue crayon, waiting for him to reach out and take it again. With the mind of a predator just waiting for the prey, I remained silent. No more warnings were coming. I had made my point and I was serious. No one would take what was mine and no one would disrespect me, fourth grader or not.

Then it happened. He reached for the crayon. I took my pencil that I had been sharpening for several minutes, making it as sharp as a weapon, and with everything I had, with all my might, I stabbed him right in the fucking forearm as he reached for my crayon. "I told you, fucker, don't touch my shit!"

He turned white as a ghost as the blood began to shoot from his wound, and he screamed so loudly that the teacher rushed over and was clearly in shock. She screamed at me, "Why did you do that?"

I said, very calmly, "He stole my blue crayon."

I felt at that moment completely empowered. It was one of the first times I had ever felt that way. Control through fear. That worked well, I thought.

Of course, I was thrown out of class and sent to the principal's office to sit for hours while they called my parents. I'll never forget my principal because he taught us the difference between "principal" and "principle" this way. "Always remember that I am your principal, and you can remember how to spell that because I am your 'pal.' A principal is always your pal," he would say. I wondered if that would hold true on this day because I was pretty scared about the consequences of my actions.

My mother arrived at the school. I was hoping my father would be at work and couldn't or wouldn't come. Holy shit, I thought, What will I do when he finds out? After another hour of my mother being in the office with my "pal" and me having to wait outside, I was terrified at what might be the outcome. My mother came storming out of the office, and I will never forget what she said to the principal walking out.

"Why the hell did that boy take my son's crayon in the first place?"

Wow! Did I hear that right? Was she backing me up?

That only lasted until we got home, but it was pretty cool in the moment. Publicly it was *Don't fuck with my son* and *He can do no wrong,* but privately things were different, especially when my father got home.

I can recall other times when I had gotten into a fight at school and my father would ask me if I hurt the other guy really bad. I'd say, "Yes, I think I got some really good shots in," and that would be followed up with him saying, "Okay, now go to your room, and we will talk about this later." Sometimes, later never came. My father would get extremely pissed off at the little things and not so pissed off at the major or violent things. Especially when it came to self-defense. This was very confusing as a child because if I broke something all hell would break loose but if I stabbed someone, it was, "Well, I'm sure there was a good reason for the stabbing."

My father grew up in a really rough neighborhood. He eventually went on to join the military after graduation just to get the hell out of that neighborhood. He would tell me stories of how he had to fight off a few jerkoffs daily just to walk from his house to the public school. Finally, he taught me how he was able to accomplish it a little easier. He told me how he would carry an umbrella to school every day. It didn't matter if it was raining or not, he would have his umbrella. You see, at school, they won't take away your umbrella if you think it might rain. Well, my dad thought it might rain every day. He told me how he had taken an umbrella that had a really hard metal tip at the end, and he'd spent days sharpening this tip until it was perfected. Perfectly sharpened and ready to use, in case of rain, of course.

One day, he was walking to school, and a couple of guys started to make fun of him. "It's a sunny day, you asshole. Hey, you dumb fuck, I'm talking to you." Here came the loudmouth and a few of his tough guy buddies.

"Why do you have an umbrella?" he said.

"In case it rains."

"It's sunny as shit out, you moron! You got any money on you?" they asked.

The tough guy began to walk up to my dad as the rest of his crew began to laugh. This guy was so stupid not to see what was coming. He got right up close in my dad's face and told him to hand over his money.

My dad said, "Sure, I've got it right here for you." He reached down, flipped the umbrella up, and put the sharpened end up to this jerkoff's neck. With the point resting on the tough guy's carotid artery, he said, "I'm sorry, what is it you need again?" The tough guy's crew wasn't very protective of their leader because they ran away, leaving the tough guy to fend for himself.

The tough guy begged for forgiveness at this point, and the way I was told the story was that forgiveness was granted. I'm not sure that is how the story really ended, but I was young, and my mom was in the room when I was being told this story giving my dad the evil eye, as if to say This story better have a happy ending. My dad told his principal or "pal" that he thought it was going to rain that day and every day thereafter.

This crayon incident set off an interesting set of events. First, I learned my family had somewhat of a Mafia mentality, which made perfect sense given that we are all first- and second-generation Italians. The Mafia's code is that no one under any circumstances can hurt a "made" member of the family, except for another "made" member in the same family, and even then, you must have permission from the leader of that family. In other words, we are allowed to punish our own, but if an outsider tries that shit, they are dead. It makes no difference who's right and who's wrong.

Second, the school initially wanted to expel me for the incident and seriously considered it, but I was a straight "A" student, so they decided to give me a battery of tests to determine my intelligence level. They wanted to see if I could distinguish right from wrong and a few other things. The only result of these tests that I ever got was that I was too smart to be expelled. The superintendent of schools forbade someone of my intelligence to be expelled for (what they reduced down to) "fighting." Therefore, I was given another chance to stay in school, and they moved my seat away from the kid I'd stabbed.

There was a lot of Mafia talk in my family, which is all a hundred percent Italian, quite large, and "off the boat," as they say. My mom was one of eight kids who grew up in a very small house in a not-so-good neighborhood. My father had a similar set of circumstances but with fewer siblings.

I have to give them credit for getting out of there and getting us into a middle-class neighborhood, even if we could barely afford to live in it.

Every Sunday, we would go back to that tiny house, where the whole family would gather for dinner once a week. It was there I would overhear things the men in my family would say about the Mafia. When I asked my mother, "Who are these Mafia people?" she said, "Oh, they are people who help Italians come to America." They sound like nice people, I thought. Maybe I could help people like they do one day when I'm older. Everyone seemed to have so much respect for them. What I didn't know at that time was that it was respect through fear.

CHAPTER 4:

What Is Your Why?

I got my first job at the age of eleven. My friends and I all used to hang out at a local pizza place after school because it had all the cool video games back then. I can't remember a time when we as a family had extra money growing up. My father, however, had a great work ethic. I got that from him. You must work, you must make money, you must support your family! This is what a real man does. Those are actually very good life lessons that have served me well over the years. I try to pass that down to my children in a slightly less sexist way. A real woman can make money as well.

I thought that since we all went to this particular pizza place to hang out and play video games, I might as well get paid for being there. Why not work where we hung out? So one day, I walked in like I owned the pizza place. I felt sure I was giving this restaurant owner an opportunity to employ me! With the utmost confidence, I asked him to hire me, thinking he was going to jump at the chance to have someone like me on his payroll. Apparently, I thought very highly of myself. Like I was the answer to all his restaurant needs. I walked up to him with my chest out and head high, looking him right in the eye, and I said, "I want to work here."

He looked at me, puzzled. "Like are you for real?"

"Yes, sir," I said.

"What can you do for me?"

"Absolutely anything you need."

"I don't need anything," he replied.

I wasn't prepared for that. "You must need something done in here."

He said with certainty, "We have it all covered between me and the other guy who works here."

I was devastated. How could he turn me down? I was so sure he was going to open up his checkbook on the spot and say something like, "Yes, Ray, when can you start?"

Needless to say, I wasn't giving up that easily. I went in there every single day after school and asked him every single day for 166 days straight to give me a job, skipping only the days when there wasn't any school. This guy was probably having nightmares about me showing up to his business daily and demanding work.

Eventually, one Saturday night, I was with all my friends having a great time, and we were going to head over to someone's house to hang out because their parents weren't home. On our way to the party, we stopped in at the pizzeria to get some food. I remember that I couldn't wait to get to the party that night, as I had been very excited about it all week.

The owner of the restaurant seemed quite different on this particular day. He was clearly exhausted. I ordered a slice of pizza and he said to me, "Hey kid, you still want a job?"

"Hell, yes," I said.

"Great. Can you start right now?"

"You mean now? I'm on my way to a party. It's Saturday night."

How dare he ask me to work at the last minute? What was he thinking? I gave him so many chances to hire me, and now he wants to ruin my Saturday night? I looked over at all my friends who were all so excited to go to the party. They were calling me: "Let's go, Ray!"

The boss said, "If you say no now, don't ever ask me again."

I asked, "What would I have to do?" He took me into the back-kitchen area and showed me the biggest pile of dirty pots, pans, and dishes I had ever seen in my life. It went from floor to ceiling. There had to be at least seventy-five pieces that needed washing. "How much will you pay me?" I asked.

"One dollar an hour, but it will be off the books. That's what I pay everyone."

"I'll take it!"

"Great. You can start right now. Here is an apron."

I went outside and told my friends to go to the party without me. I had a job, and I was a real man now. It took me four hours to do those dishes, so I got home really late for an eleven-year-old.

"Where the heck were you?" Mom said this with my dad there in the room as well.

I was so excited to give them the answer, I knew they would be pleased. I was so proud to tell them I was working, that I had a real job, and I was now a man.

"I work at the pizza place now," I said, proud as hell.

They were kind of shocked. My father asked, "How much do you make?"

I said again, very proudly, "One dollar per hour."

"What!!!" my dad said. He was furious. "You work for how much? He kept you there until almost midnight working for a dollar an hour? That is ridiculous. You can't work for a dollar an hour. That is pathetic. He is taking advantage of you. Why would you allow that? Are you stupid or something? I'm going up there to straighten his ass out!"

I was completely devastated, crushed, and humiliated. I begged my father not to go there. I would certainly lose the job that had taken me almost six months to get. All I wanted was to hear was, "Good job, son." He could have followed that up with something to the effect of, "That salary is below minimum wage, which isn't allowed by law, but I appreciate your efforts."

He didn't go up there to straighten my boss's ass out like he said he would, but he was clearly very disappointed in me. I'd been sure he was going to be so proud of his son. I would carry the anger I felt that day with me for most of my life. I would show him how great I was. I would show my father that I was even better than him. I would be more successful than he could ever be. I kept that job until the place finally went out of business, sometimes working twelve-hour shifts at eleven years old for twelve dollars a day. I took pride in myself and in my work regardless of what anyone thought. Since that day, I have always had a job. I also went on to earn a salary that was ten times higher than my father's highest annual salary ever was. Anger fueled that fire and desire for success.

Anything positive that is extremely difficult for us to accomplish in life is usually triggered by a deep-rooted feeling or emotion. It was relatively recent when one of my business competitors came to me to try to recruit me to work for his company instead of the one I was currently working for. We sat in a local diner; he bought us lunch and then he asked me the following question.

"What is your why?"

I repeated back his question to him, as I was somewhat confused by what he meant, "What is my why? I don't understand the question."

"Why do you do what you do for a living, and why are you successful at it?"

Now I see where he is going with this question, I thought. Here was my answer.

"I do it so my kids have everything they need and some of the things they want. That is my why. If my employer paid me in all the things my kids need and some of what they want, I would be just fine with that. I wouldn't need money because that is what I will use it for, and that is my why," I proudly exclaimed.

My lunch buddy nearly dropped his coffee.

He said, "I have asked that question to over a hundred people and every one of them said it was for the money, success, or both."

"I assure you I am not everyone," I said. I only take what I need from the universe and just a little extra for comfort, and I leave the rest. I am not greedy. I don't believe in greed. I have always lived this way, and I have always gotten what I needed from the universe and often a little more. Even in the worst of times or depressions and recessions, somehow, I succeeded.

This was a trick question. Money is always the wrong answer here. What you will do with the money and the emotional driving force behind the acquisition of such is. Let me explain why.

The love that I have for my children is an emotion that is so powerful it will make me do anything to succeed and get them what they need. That love or emotion is far too powerful for me not to succeed. The emotion for any success, or to accomplish any goal in life, can vary, but it must be a serious, intense, emotional drive that carries you toward the goal you seek. Do you really think for one second there is anything I wouldn't do for the well-being of my children? Nothing can stop me with a why like that.

My first emotion was anger. Anger towards my father. This fueled me by not being considered good enough: I'll show you! That type of thing. Anger can be a very strong and powerful motivator. Later in life, however, the emotion became love. The love for my kids. That being said, if you wish to succeed, you need to have that deep-rooted emotion to drive you and push you forward each time you get down or frustrated or think about giving up. We must go back deep into our minds to our why, and that will make us push through every time.

Logic can help you make good, intelligent, and rational choices, but it is only an emotion from deep within you that will push you through the worst shit that life can ever throw at you—one that will get you to your goal on the other side of a complete shit storm without fear of injury or death. If you are willing to die for your why, nothing can stop you

Let me repeat that because it is one of the most important things in this entire book: **If you are willing to die for your why, nothing can stop you.**

So then, why can't you say something like, "Well, my emotion will be happiness once I'm rich"? Simple, because nothing could be further from the truth. Your brain knows this. You can't trick your subconscious mind into believing that a $200,000 car is more important than a $20,000 car. Both will get you from point A to point B, and your subconscious mind knows this. Are you willing to die for a $200,000 car? If not, then it's not your why, and that's not a strong enough emotion. Find something you will die for. Find a real, true, deep-rooted, psychological, emotional reason for accomplishing something and attach it to your goal, and there will be nothing, and I mean nothing, that can stop you from achieving it.

CHAPTER 5:

Trauma; It's What's for Dinner

1. Becoming Fearless. I was a very young teenager when I was first touched by a woman in a sexual manner. I had no idea what to expect. I was probably looking for love or companionship. The woman touching me was almost twice my age. What she saw in me, I have no idea. I guess she saw a very confused young person who wanted to be loved, and she capitalized on that. In hindsight, this was sexual abuse, but I didn't understand that back then. She was a predator, and I was the prey.

She would pick me up and bring me somewhere. She drove; I was too young to drive. Sometimes her place, sometimes the car, sometimes a friend's place. If I didn't feel like participating, they would both berate me until I gave in. They would always get very intoxicated before commencing anything. It became a ritual of sorts. I would indulge in the drinking as well to numb myself.

I remember another woman who used to invite me over to go swimming at her house. She wasn't twice my age but old enough to be in college, and I was really young. She lived with her parents and would only have me there during the day when they were at work. The first time she invited me over, I really thought we were going to go swimming! How naïve I must have been. I didn't even get my fucking swim suit on. I don't know if I found these women or they found me, but somehow, we found each other. My difficulties with older women were just beginning.

I have successfully repressed much of these memories. I am not saying this is a good thing, nor do I recommend it, but my memory of these incidents is quite limited today because that is what I had to do to move past them. I boxed them up in my mind and buried the box down deep below many other boxes of memories that were horrible in nature so they couldn't affect me. At least that is what I thought. Later in life, I would learn that these memories would come back to cause me much grief. Trauma lives forever in your nervous system, and when we are faced with something that triggers the memory, we snap. That is the basis of post-traumatic stress disorder, or PTSD.

I certainly don't want anyone to feel sorry for me, as it was these and other events that made me as strong as I am today. I know for a fact that I am fully capable of overcoming any adversity. Absolutely anything! Without any tragedies or trauma, how could I know that?

I remember reading a particular book about business. The author explained something so profound I held on to it forever, and I think it applies to all things, not just business. He explained in his book that you can and will learn much more from your losses than your wins in life. In other words, if you open a business and everything goes perfectly and the business is a huge success, you won't learn nearly as much as the person who has had a business that struggled to survive and eventually became successful or perhaps even went out of business. This is so true in all aspects of life.

Think about the people you know who have had an easy life. They have not had to make tough choices and decisions and learn from them. It's the tragedies and disasters in life we learn the most from, not the successes, especially if they come easy. The more difficult the experience, the stronger you can become. So, the next time you are looking at what may feel like the worst possible thing to ever happen to you, just remember this: it is that experience that will one day make you fearless. You can't be limitless until you are fearless.

2. Learning Manifestation. It was the late 1980s, and I had a rather good job for myself where I was doing well and moving up the ladder of success. My boss was pretty cool. We got along, and it seemed he had my back. He was grooming me for a promotion, but I had to pay my dues first, so to speak. I had no problem with that. I'd do what I had to do to get to the next level. He and I worked together for a while until one day he came in with this woman and his boss to deliver some news to me.

The news was that my boss was leaving the company, and this woman was going to take his place as my new boss. Now I was pissed because I would have to start all over again with this new supervisor and prove myself all over again to get a promotion, one that had been promised to me and was only a few months away. I asked him, "How could you do this? How could you do this to me? Did you explain to this new person what the plan is for my future?"

Later on, I realized he was getting fired, not resigning, and his replacement certainly had not been made aware of all the things I had done to get promoted. I was starting from scratch all over again. I spoke to my new boss and explained what I was promised. I explained that I really needed this job and the promotion because we really needed the money. We always needed money. Telling her how very important this job was to me would prove later on, however, to be a very big mistake.

She agreed to "test me out" and see "how I would perform" if I was given that promotion. Basically, I would do the job without officially having the title or the salary. I agreed to do it. As this particular new job would require a lot of traveling on my part, it came with hotel and travel expenses, but I did not officially have the job, so she had to make all of my travel arrangements for me, including my hotel stays.

One day before I left for a trip, she said to me, "I booked a double room with two beds to save money because I have to come out there also."

I was fucking stunned. Really? Is this really happening to me? Am I going to have to fuck this bitch for my promotion?

I'm sure we have all had sexual experiences that we did not want to have, but for men this is different. Many people falsely believe that a man must be aroused in order to get an erection and/or ejaculate, and if a man does have an erection, he must be willingly participating and enjoying the sexual experience. This is not the case. In fact, even slight genital stimulation or even stress for that matter can cause erections, even when no specific sexual stimulation is present. An erection does not mean that a man consents to or wants to have sex.

These experiences changed me. I was never going to be the same again. I was never going to give another human being that type of sexual control over me. I felt right then that I had to take that power back one woman at a time. All of my sexual encounters from that time forward were on my terms and were always with women older than I. The tables were turned. I wanted to feel that power and dominance. I became somewhat predatory, and any female in her thirties or forties could be my prey. I would go out regularly and look for who would be my next sexual conquest. Of course, all sexual acts were consensual. It had to be this way to fulfill my needs. They each had to agree to fully submit themselves to me. No phone numbers ever, no last names, and they would never see me again. Why I thought that these sexual encounters with strangers were going to make me feel better I'm not sure, but I definitely felt as though I had regained control.

More often than not, I just wanted to leave their house once I had gotten them back there, long before having sex. I had already achieved my goal at that point. I didn't need to actually have the sex. That's because this was never about the sex for me. This was never about hurting anyone. It was about me regaining control.

Needless to say, it didn't take long thereafter for me to be completely disgusted with my "new job" and my new boss. One day, I recall running into an old friend from high school. I noticed he was spending money like it was completely expendable, so I asked him, "What have you done to make all this money?"

He went on to explain how he had had a car accident and sued the other driver, who had caused the accident, for a lot of money. This was back in the days when car accident lawsuits were very lucrative. Today, there are many laws that prevent this type of frivolous lawsuit unless you are very seriously injured and bedridden.

Instantly, the wheels in my brain began spinning. I became consumed with thoughts of my past driving experiences and which ones would result in an accident that would not be my fault and where I would get hurt but not enough to die. Day after day, each time I got into my car, I had these intense thoughts of being in an accident.

It was a rainy Tuesday morning, and I was driving my car to work. I was driving down the middle lane of the highway, and there was a car in the right lane next to me just a few feet ahead of me. This guy decided to change lanes and move into my lane without looking. Obviously, had he checked his mirror, he would have known I was there. He began to change lanes, and I lay on my horn. Just as he was inches away from hitting me, he realized his mistake and swerved back into his lane without causing a collision. I was livid. My heart was racing. My adrenaline was pumping through my body like fire running through my veins. I wanted to kill this idiot. I pulled alongside him to curse him out and call him every name in the book. (By the way, who wrote this infamous book on name calling, anyway?) I was looking directly at him through my passenger side window while I was driving, so he would know I was pissed off at him. What I failed to see was that directly in front of me, about one hundred yards away, the traffic had come to a complete halt. Just seconds before the impact I thought, "Holy shit, I am going to die!"

I slammed on the brakes at about sixty miles per hour and skidded fifteen feet into the rear end of the car in front of me. The car behind me drove into me at what felt like the same speed. The next car rear-ended him, causing me to take another hit, which made me hit my head and almost black out. My car was then pushed into the left lane, where I was struck again by another oncoming car and then that car was hit by the one behind him, resulting in me taking four more hits. I placed my hands over my face and head like a boxer who is up against the ropes trying to protect himself. I crouched down under the steering wheel, begging God or anyone to make this stop. I couldn't get hit again, but it seemed like it would never stop.

My car was now facing the wrong way on a one-way highway hanging half off the divider in the middle of the road. I was in and out of consciousness. I heard someone screaming my name and I came to. With my eyes barely open, I could see a female officer, and I heard her say, "Is he with

31

us?" This was a polite way of her asking the paramedics if I was dead. I couldn't speak, but I was able to raise one finger. They had to cut me out of the car. I was placed in traction at the scene and remained that way for a very long time.

On a lighter note, do you know how people say, "Make sure you're wearing clean underwear in case you have an accident?" Well, it was laundry day for me, and although I did have on clean underwear, it was the very last pair that I owned, which I would never wear unless it was the only pair that was clean. This is because they were given to me as a joke by a girlfriend on Valentine's Day. By now, I am sure you have a visual of some of that silly underwear they make for men. These were some sort of animal print in black and white. Good God, can I catch a break?

The very first thing they did at the hospital was cut off all my clothes. At this point, I was still in shock and the pain had not set in. All I could think about was that stupid frigging underwear I was wearing. "At least they are clean," I said to the nurse. She seemed unamused, as she had more import-ant things to worry about, which scared the shit out of me because those things had to be my injuries. I just couldn't feel them or see them yet.

When the pain set in, it was like a bomb went off inside me. Everything hurt at once. I screamed for them to get me out of the traction device. I couldn't take it anymore, but they could not let me out of it until they knew my back wasn't broken. They also refused to give me pain medicine until all my injuries could be identified. After hours, or what seemed like hours, I was finally released from traction, which made me feel slightly better. I was given instructions and a prescription for something and eventually released.

Other than cuts, bruises, and a serious concussion, they said I hadn't bro-ken anything.

I had some permanent injuries to my neck and back that were discovered later through medical testing. They continue to bother me to this day. I got myself an amazing lawyer who specialized in this type of thing. I really didn't get a lot of money from the lawsuit, especially since I'd hit the first car. It was not worth it in retrospect, and I don't recommend trying this.

Two realizations came from this. The first is that you can manifest anything in your life that you want, both positive and negative, so be very careful what you ask for. Remember, I wanted the accident so I didn't have to deal with my job. The second thing was that I somehow managed to survive a horrific accident. Even the police thought I was dead on site. It has always seemed that at my darkest hour someone or something was there to save me. Why was that?

3. Becoming the Perfect Storm. After recovering from the accident, I was out of a job and needed work. I didn't have much of a resume, as I hadn't finished college. A friend of a friend introduced me to a businessman who owned and operated many types of businesses. Many were in the hospitality industry, and the primary requirement was loyalty.

Let's call him Vinny, though this is not his actual name. Vinny had a large organization that was always looking for people. Vinny had plenty of legitimate businesses that were expanding rapidly. Everyone's job was to protect these businesses. That wasn't the job title, but it was part of the job. Everyone was given a "regular" job, so to speak, and was expected to keep their mouths shut and remain loyal. I was highly qualified for my job, and I was very good at it.

Vinny had competitors just like any business does, but in his world, when one company wanted to acquire another company, the term hostile takeover took on an entirely different meaning. I was unaware that a competitor wanted to take over one such business—the one I was standing in.

This business was a bar. After hours one night, at around four or five in the morning, Vinny and bunch of guys were hanging around drinking at the bar. I was done for the night and about to leave, but I stopped to drop off a bunch of glasses behind the bar that I had picked up on route to leaving for the night, and this is when the guys sitting around began to ask me for drinks. I only knew a few of these people, so I looked at Vinny and he gave me a head nod as if to say it was okay to serve them drinks. I knew better than to do anything without Vinny's head nod. No one did anything without getting the head nod or the okay to do something, even if it was as small a task as serving a drink.

I am not a bartender, but what these types of guys drink is really simple for me or anyone to make because they drink from bottle to glass. There aren't any additional ingredients required. The only thing you need to know when pouring for them is whether they want it on the rocks or neat. This is bar lingo which means with or without ice. These were real drinkers. They wanted to kill as many brain cells as possible in the quickest time possible. Nothing fruity ever went into their drinks; they were never likely to order flavored martinis at a late-night sit down among associates.

Everyone was acting like they were having a good time, but the tension in there could be cut with a knife. On one side of the bar was a drug dealer. By the way, never trust a drug dealer. They will turn on anyone in heartbeat. They have no true loyalty whatsoever, and their word is meaningless. If taking someone down builds them up, they will hurt anyone to do it. Perhaps you have to be that way in their business. On the other side of the bar was Vinny and some associates I had never seen before.

The voice inside me was the same one I have heard throughout most of my life when something bad is coming. The voice that is never wrong. It said loud and clear, "Get out of there. Go out the side door. Go now!"

As I was about to leave, the drug dealer yelled out to me, "Hey Ray, give me a Johnnie Walker on the rocks." Of course, I looked over at Vinny for the nod first, and once I had his approval, I reached for the bottle of Johnnie Red. The dealer shouted back, "Don't give me that shit. Give me the Johnnie Black." Once again, I got the nod because the Johnnie Black is far more expensive than Red. Then, what followed was the stupidest joke I had heard so many times working in bars. Some idiot at the bar yelled out, "What the hell is the difference between Johnnie Red and Johnnie Black?" Everyone else in unison at the bar yelled, "Twelve years, you fucking idiot. Hahaha!" I will never forget this joke as long as I live and you'll read why in a moment. I simply bent down to get the Johnnie Walker Black out of the cabinet where it is kept locked up right next to the Johnnie Blue, which, if this guy had any real class, he would have asked for since the Blue is much more expensive than the Black.

While I was low to the ground behind the bar, everyone else was on the other side laughing and pretending to like one another, when suddenly I heard, "Pop, Pop, Pop, Pop." This sounded like firecrackers going off indoors, but I knew better. I know all too well what gunshots sound like. I couldn't see anything from my location behind the bar, so I had no idea who shot at whom. At this point, my ears went dead, and I couldn't hear anything. They seemed to have stopped working. My eyes were wide open, and my body was completely trembling from head to toe, filled with adrenaline rushing through my veins. I needed to think quickly, but I couldn't seem to move. At that point, I heard the familiar voice inside me saying, "Side door." The thing was, to get to that door, I knew I would be seen, and I had nothing to defend myself with except for a bottle of Johnnie Black in my right hand, a bottle of Johnnie Red in the other, along with the element of surprise because I doubted anyone had remembered that I was bent down behind the bar.

The first door I had to get to was about ten feet away, but the second door to the street outside was much farther, maybe another forty feet away, and I would have had to double back through a long corridor to get there, giving the shooter enough time to chase me out the first door and possibly get me with a long shot. So, even if I got through the first door, I may not have made it to the second. My car was parked right outside that second door, facing in the direction of the street. It was almost as if I had known when I parked it that I might need to get away fast that night. I had never parked there before. If I had parked in my usual assigned parking space, I might never have made it to my car. This entire plan of my getting away was contingent on my assumption that, somehow, I could fight my way through the first door. Four shots had been fired, which meant in a revolver there would have to be two shots left. If it was a semiautomatic, then there could be six or eleven shots left depending on the size of the magazine. Back in those days, you could still purchase a fifteen-round magazine. Today, they are outlawed.

I was in complete survival mode. I am no hero in this story. I was petrified and trying to get the fuck out of there alive. Everything relayed until this point took about fifteen to thirty seconds in real time, from the shooting to making my escape route, in my head, guided by an unknown source "speaking to me" the entire time.

My final thought as I began to stand upright was, This is it! It's go time. If I die, I will fight to the fucking death. Just me and Johnnie Walker. And with that, I stood up and I completely blacked out.

I didn't pass out, mind you, I blacked out. This has happened to me many times previously in bouts of rage or trauma. There is a block of time missing from my memory, from the time I began to stand up to the next memory I have of sitting inside my car outside the building with my hands shaking uncontrollably trying to get the car key into the ignition. This stands out because on the first attempt I dropped the keys on the car floor and I may have screamed. I'm not sure if that scream was only in my head or real and out loud because I still couldn't hear anything, but I continued trying to pick up the keys, while praying I could get the fucking car to start and get out of there. I do not remember the actual drive home, nor do I remember what I did once there.

Many years later, while I was working with a PTSD counselor, I tried to recollect the events of that night, as well as others, but I was unable to, nor did I actually want to. She suggested hypnosis, but I really didn't want to know. I believe that the blackouts are a part of me protecting me. I believe that the human mind does this specifically to keep oneself from going crazy from significant life-threatening traumas. I can't recall the details of most of my traumas.

Today, I hate alcoholic beverages, but especially Johnnie Walker. It's been over thirty years since that event, and even today, if I so much as see a bottle of Johnnie Walker, I begin to tremble inside.

This is unfortunately only one of several incidents like this in my life, but as a result of them, I was becoming the perfect storm.

Ask yourself right now: Can you weather any storm? Can you handle the absolute worst shit life can throw at you? Can you handle the types of things that would bring anyone else to the breaking point of their existence? If you can weather that storm, you then become the fucking storm and your power is beautiful.

4. Sex, Drugs, and Rock-n-Roll. I was in search of a new way to make some serious money, and I was consumed with the thoughts of how best to do so. I began running various scenarios through my mind of how badly I wanted an abundance of money and what exactly I was willing to do for it. There was always a desperate need for it, and I was sick of dealing with this issue. I had a serious moral dilemma. I knew there were several illegal ways to make money, and I certainly considered them, but they went against everything my "gut" was telling me. Even back then I believed in Karma.

I saw a friend who told me there was quite a bit of money to be made working in nightclubs as a disc jockey. I kind of knew this already, especially being in the New York area club scene. As a DJ, I could do very well without crossing the lines that I wanted to stay clear of, such as illegal activities. However, this work was not easy to break into as an unknown. To get this type of job, first, you needed to be really good at it, and second, you needed someone to help "get you in" and be heard in order to have any chance of getting hired. My friend was able to help me with both.

This began one of the worst chapters of my life that I am the least proud of. Taking into consideration the type of person I was at this point in time, an obsessive extremist with an addictive personality, giving me the opportunity to make a lot of money and be around countless women and an unlimited supply of drugs and alcohol was, needless to say, a recipe for a life-altering disaster. I overindulged in everything this fucked-up lifestyle had to offer. All night drug-and alcohol-induced parties were a regular occurrence. I was broken before I got into this life, and by the time I got out, I was completely fucking demolished.

I found myself in rehab for drugs and alcohol, and I had become one of "those people." The ones you talk about and look down on until you realize you ARE one!

It may have appeared to outsiders like it was fun and everyone was having a grand old time, but this was the absolute lowest point of my existence. Being completely covered up and masked with self-medicating experiences and fake happiness; I was lonely, depressed, and had no direction or path. It was a hollow existence.

Why do you suppose I used intoxicants? It is a product one uses to temporarily alter one's perception of their individual reality.

What if one found a process to change the perception of oneself within their true reality? What if this process could manifest permanent positive changes in one's reality?

Would there then still be a desire to alter the perception of such temporarily?

I'm happy to say that I have never used drugs or alcohol again, and with complete clarity, I can assure you that life without them is extraordinary.

Your past is just a story, and once you realize this, it has no power over you. Remember, the best views of the world come after the hardest climb.

CHAPTER 6:

The Beginning of the Light

I always knew I had great intuition. I had the ability to foresee the immediate future or gain information about someone, such as whether they were lying or being truthful. Later in life, however, this ability began to grow exponentially and branched off in different directions. For example, I began knowing very personal and intimate details about people that I had recently met. These thoughts or feelings just randomly began to pop into my mind. At least at the time, I thought they were completely random. More on that later.

I would also get warnings that protected me from bad shit or accidents. For example, I always seemed to know when to stop my car from driving forward because another car was about to speed through a stop sign while not paying attention to what was in front of him. Had I not listened to those warnings, I would have been involved in what could have been major automobile accidents. These warnings kept me safe. I didn't know why or who they were from, but they got me out of trouble many times. They stopped me from doing stupid, reckless things in my younger years. I would immediately get a message of STOP! Then I might "see" the outcome or sometimes the potential consequences in my mind before I did something that would prove to be dangerous for me. I knew of no reason why someone up there was looking out for me. I had no faith or belief in anything spiritual. Nonetheless, I was getting information that saved my ass many times, and I was grateful for it.

At some point in my late twenties, other strange occurrences began to happen from time to time. While completely alone, I would hear a word out of nowhere. I would hear it and then I'd forget it. I had not been able to figure out why that was. Where was it coming from? I would frantically look in every room of my apartment, because I was wondering who the heck was in my home. Then I checked all the televisions, electronics, and any items that could make a sound, but they were always turned off. Since for some reason I could never seem to remember the word, I was never able to utilize this ability. My medium teacher years later, taught me this was a "word drop," which refers to hearing one or two words at any moment in time for a specific reason. The reason was left up to me to figure out.

It was in this very same apartment that I first saw the "lines." You may have seen these yourself, and just disregarded them. Let me explain. These lines appear in our peripheral vision and seem to shoot though the air and disappear in a split second. If you try to look at them straight on, you can't see them. This particular apartment had many different "lines" that would come around from time to time and visit.

I believe these lines to be the energy of people no longer on this Earth. (Later on, I will explain how I learned this and the science behind it.) I would see the line and then "feel" a change in the energy in the room. I would feel a vibration, and it felt like something was there, like I wasn't alone. I am sure you can relate to this feeling. It is one where you feel like you are being watched. The energy can arrive with low vibrations or high vibrations. The combination of the vibrations and the lines is how I know I am being paid a visit from the other side. I would later learn that the low vibrations meant there was something serious in nature trying to be relayed to me, and the lighter, higher vibrations meant that it was more pleasant in nature.

But just imagine me for one second. I am in my new apartment, I am a swinging, single bachelor in my mid-to-late twenties who just wants to work, make money, and meet girls, and every time I come home, I see speeding lines, feel energies, and hear words drop out of the sky while I am at home on my own. I was really beginning to doubt my sanity. Let me add something else to the mix. Since I was avoiding these energies, they would fuck with my electrical appliances to get my attention. The burglar alarm was their favorite. I imagine they somehow knew I was the hyper-vigilant type who would notice when something turned my alarm system on and off. I must have had the poor maintenance man fix this damn alarm a hundred times.

He would keep telling me, "Nothing is wrong with it. It works perfectly."

"Just look at it again!"

The telephone was the other thing. These energies had a grand old time with the old-fashioned landline telephones we used to have—on and off, ring and stop, cutting off conversations. I was once on the phone telling my friend jokingly that I thought my apartment was haunted when the phone suddenly went dead. And bear in mind that at this point in my life, I still continued to rationalize and disbelieve any and all of this was real.

Let us fast forward to some twenty-something years after I lived in that apartment. This is when the next monumental paranormal event took place and when things really got intense.

This is not to imply that there wasn't any other unexplainable crazy shit transpiring in those, in between years, but I would never accept them as reality as of yet and I doubt you'll want to read a 1000-page autobiography about me.

This next discovery was the biggest one of them all and most certainly the least believable. These were the messages coming from the other side.

"People," for lack of a better word, were starting to send me messages. These people were not in the same room as me. They were not in the same building as me. They were not even in the same realm of existence as me because they were all dead! Sounds crazy, right? That's because it is fucking crazy! This whole life experience of mine has been crazy. It's difficult to even tell this story. I often stop myself writing it and say something like, "This is frigging crazy, Ray! No one is ever going to believe this! Stop writing before they lock you up and throw away the key!"

This new phenomenon (new to me, anyway) was the next level after what had happened in that apartment some twenty plus years earlier. It took me that long to make the connection. Here's how it works. The lines make themselves visible for just a split second. With the lines comes the feeling of vibrations around me and then the feeling I am not alone. If I focus on the energy and allow my mind to drift off or go into a type of meditative or altered state, what comes next will blow your mind. At least, it certainly did mine.

I began to get actual messages from them, and they appear on what looks a bit like a movie screen. This is the only way I can describe it. The people in the movie may be among the living, except for one, and that is the one bringing me the message. I can typically only see parts of people, and rarely if ever an entire person. I will see the image of the person from either the bust up to the top of their head or from the waist down. Sometimes it may be their back or their side facing me. The message is usually like a short video loop. So, for example, the dead person will say perhaps, one or two sentences, and the scene will repeat itself over and over. It can take me a while to figure out who all the people are. Very often, I have never met those people who are communicating with me, nor do I have any direct knowledge of them or their existence. However, there is usually a common person between myself and the deceased. I will explain this more later. The messages are often more important to someone other than me as well. I guess the dead know they can come through me, so to speak, and hope that I will give their message to the appropriate living being.

Some of the dead are extremely persistent and very annoying. They will often not leave me alone until I share their message. In one case, I got very strong and serious low vibrations followed by the same eight-second "video" loop in my head for an entire four days. By the end of the fourth day, I was utterly livid because I couldn't turn it off. Once I figured out who the message was for and delivered it, everything went away in an instant—the movie screen, the low vibrations in my body, everything just went as if it had never been there.

Keep in mind that when I say I "see" something or "hear" something, I'm using those terms for lack of a better word. I don't actually see dead people with my eyes, nor do I hear them with my ears. Everything is entirely telepathic. It originates in their consciousness (which is still very active without a body) and is sent into my consciousness. Forget the movies you have seen on television. It isn't like that at all. You can't actually see them or hear them with your eyes and ears. At least I cannot anyway. The day I do, I will run out and get a prescription.

Another ability that came to me later was the ability to know about another person through their own thoughts. The person can be living in this realm or not, and they typically must be thinking about or obsessing over the subject matter for me to obtain it. It always helps if I can see a picture of the person. I can often look at a picture of someone and gain a good amount of information about them. Sometimes I am able to relay their plans for the next day if they are dwelling on it. I am admittedly not very good at initiating the "grabbing" of someone's thoughts. More often, they are just given to me for some reason that I cannot yet explain. About ninety-five percent of my abilities up until this point in time just "come" to me. I do not initiate or go out to get them. Initiating is something I plan to learn in the near future. I believe it is a skill that must be developed through practice over time.

Free will, which we all have, allows any of us the ability to change our minds at any time, which is why I never claim to have the ability to predict the future with total accuracy. However, if someone is thinking about something a lot, I can pick it up like an antenna picks up UHF television. (UHF television broadcasting is the use of ultra-high frequency for over-the-air transmission of television signals) It's a lot like that, actually. Remember the old-fashioned televisions that had UHF? We would try to tune in to a TV show that was on UHF, but it would barely come in. It would be grainy and hard to make out what you were seeing or hearing. It is exactly like that when I am in another person's consciousness. It takes a long time to tune in and see something.

Here's how this can work. If someone, for example, is planning to go fishing tomorrow and they are consciously thinking about getting ready to go, I can sometimes pick that up. In other words, I can sometimes pick up what they may be dwelling on.

As an interesting side note, did you know that the cosmic microwave background (or CMB) that blankets the universe is responsible for a sizable amount of static on your television or radio. Therefore, before the days of cable, you could turn your television to an "in between" channel, and part of the static you'd see was the afterglow of the big bang according to NASA.

An important aspect of making any attempt to know someone's future events is the concept of free will. We live in a world where people change their minds. It is very possible that a man planned to go fishing the next day, thought about it, and dwelled on it, but let's say, for example, he wakes up in the morning with terrible back pain and decides to go to the doctor instead. I wouldn't necessarily be able to see that coming. That is an example of his free will and everyone has it. As long as we all have free will, the future is always changing. In fact, one change as simple as our fisherman not going fishing that day and going to the doctor can set off a chain of events that may alter several other people's lives, including his own. I call this the ripple effect.

What if our fisherman goes to the doctor that day, and in the waiting room, he meets the girl of his dreams? They get married and have two children. One of those children grows up to become the President of the United States of America and changes history. See how something as simple as not going fishing can actually change the outcome of American history? This is why I am very careful with the things I say and the things I know.

The outcome could be quite different. Let's say I see this man in his boat, and there is a storm brewing that has not yet been reported. I may be able to prevent a tragedy from happening by altering the outcome or warning the person. Later in this book, you will read about those types of events where this was a true gift for some of the people in my life, who would have been in danger otherwise. This happened more often as my skills developed over time.

Another important fact I've learned is that there is no such measurement as "time" the way we use it in other realms of existence. Time is a man-made invention to measure the length of a day, an hour, a minute, a year, etc. This man-made concept enables us to perhaps meet someone, somewhere, and both arrive together, for example. The energy beings in other realms of existence, including higher levels, do not have any use for the concept of time in this manner, and this often has consequences. If I get a message from the other side telling me something will happen, however, the giver of the message or the message itself cannot relay or reveal to me the conceptual time in which the event will occur; I therefore cannot relay the time frame in which it will happen. It may be impossible for me to figure out when that particular "something" will occur. I've seen someone I know having a serious motor vehicle accident in a premonition, but I have no idea when it will happen. So, what can I say to this person other than "drive carefully"? It is pointless telling them, as neither of us can do anything to change it if we don't know whether it will occur tomorrow or next year. Certainly, if I can prevent the accident because there is something I recognize that gives me the ability to tell when it will happen, then I will do everything I can to help that person avoid the danger.

Later, I will tell you more about one of my clairvoyant-medium teachers and advisors. The rule she taught me was very simple. Only reveal things that are in the other person's highest and best interests.

She said these exact words during the beginning of my learning process, "There are just some things you don't tell people. Some information simply shouldn't be revealed. You know what I mean Ray?"

I said, "Yes, I think I understand you perfectly."

CHAPTER 7:

Why Me?

The question of "Why me?" is the single most difficult thing for me to rationalize. If in fact all this is real, then how or why do I have these abilities? How many other people have them around the world but don't realize it? I went years without realizing it or believing it, for that matter. Are they actually a blessing or more of a curse? I think it is a double-edged sword. Knowing things you are not supposed to know is really unnerving at times.

I know this isn't life threatening or anything, but think about knowing what your significant other is thinking. I am sure you can appreciate the good and the bad that comes with this. I really could live without knowing that my girlfriend finds someone across the room attractive, for example. Or that she is pissed off at me for something I did yesterday and won't just come out and say it so I can say I'm sorry already. I swear to you I have apologized in advance for shit that I didn't get yelled at for yet. I know it's coming and try my hardest to keep my mouth shut. I really do. Would you react? Would you be able to let it go? It's actually a bit tortuous. Yes, there is definitely a downside, folks.

How about knowing intimate details of a person you just met? "Hey babe, remember the couple we met at the party the other night? Did you know they were swingers?" Or, "I think it's safe to say that Mr. Jones is definitely guilty of embezzling money from his company. Oh, and he is cheating on his wife."

This happens too often, but it is important for me to be able to "throw away" that information and allow my conscious mind the opportunity to get to know someone. It is not as easy as it sounds, I assure you, but I digress.

So let's have a closer look here. I am not particularly deserving of these gifts, at least I don't think I am necessarily. So perhaps I just found a way to "tap in" to them, so to speak. I had to go through hell and back to get mine, but I am sure many of you reading this have experienced some of these same strange events that I have (hopefully not the bad shit). Maybe you just didn't know what they were and now you do. Now, perhaps you'll be more cognizant of your gifts when you see them. I know when I'm in a room with someone who has them. What I don't know is if they know they have them, and this certainly does not make for a great conversation starter.

If you think this is what you want and you see the signs, learn to meditate. Learn really well. When I was learning to meditate in the very beginning, I could not sit still and meditate for ten minutes. Now it takes me ten minutes to enter and float around another realm. Sometimes there is nothing there and other times—well, you'll get to read about those other times soon enough.

On a much more positive note, these abilities, as I have said before, have saved my life many times. For me, I feel it is no longer necessary to ask why but rather that I should begin to accept what is and pay it forward if I can.

I think I have most likely cheated death more times than anyone on this planet. I was fairly reckless with my life decisions when I was younger, but I always came out all right. It is truly amazing. If being a teenager and thinking I was invincible wasn't enough, later, in my early twenties, I died and came back. I had a near-death experience where I went over to the "other side" and saw what death looks and feels like and returned. I have no idea why anyone would refer to this as a near-death experience. It is a real-death experience. Since I don't make the rules, we will call it a near-death. Needless to say, since that experience, I have had no fear of death whatsoever. This could have been a recipe for disaster. I was a very young man who knew he could die, and I was just fine with that because my death was actually the most beautiful experience of my life.

CHAPTER 8:

The Day of the Dawn

Let's go back in time to my late teen years. I called in sick for work the night before so I could sleep in late that morning. It may have been a weekend, because both of my parents were both at home. I was in bed feeling a little crappy in the early morning when I began to hear sirens from police cars getting closer and closer. Then I heard a lot of commotion directly under me on the first floor. The kitchen of the house was located directly under my bedroom where I was now trying to sleep, but everyone was making so much noise downstairs I figured I should check and see what was happening. I tried to lift my head but I couldn't. I could not lift my head off the pillow. This was the first sign that something was very wrong.

The noises got louder downstairs and people were yelling. I had to get up, but I couldn't move my head. This is fucking crazy. What the hell is happening to me? I couldn't yell either. I couldn't move my face. I could only move my right arm. It was the only part of my body that I could still communicate with. I used it to grab the edge of the bed and began to pull myself toward the edge, giving it everything I had. One arm worked, but nothing else. How would I get up? My legs were completely paralyzed. With my right arm, I continued to pull as hard as I could to get to the edge of the bed.

Very slowly I moved some, and then I passed out. I heard a loud clanging sound downstairs, which woke me back up. I started to pull myself toward the edge once again with my one working arm. I was pulling with every ounce of strength that I had. If I just lay there, I would be dead. This much I knew. No one was coming for me. I continued to pull, but I passed out again. Loud yelling woke me once more, and I knew this was it. I had to pull myself out of that bed.

When I finally got to the edge of the mattress, I used the same arm to begin pushing my body upright or close to it, so I thought, and then I passed out again. This time, though, I fell out of the bed. I hit the floor chin first and I was out cold. Completely unconscious. What happened next would be the defining moment of my existence.

I woke up to see what was happening. I was high up looking down at myself. I saw my father holding me and screaming for the paramedics. He must have heard me hit the floor with what would have been a loud thump. He was holding me in his arms. I was not moving. I was no longer in that body. I was above it looking down on the scene. I felt terrible that my father was suffering like this, but I also felt euphoric. I had no pain, no fears, no problems; I was just floating and feeling absolutely wonderful.

To my right was a huge cone-shaped bright white light, like I was on a stage and had the spotlight on me. Just me. I began to go deeper into the light because it felt amazing. There was something at the end of the light that I couldn't quite see, but it said, "It's okay to come into the light, Ray."

It knew my name! I looked into the light and for some strange reason, I believed this "being" when it said that the light was safe to enter, and so I proceeded to move more into it. The euphoria intensified as I went deeper into the light. Now I heard my father yelling, screaming, and crying, and I made a decision at that moment that would alter my existence forever. I said to the "being" at the end of the light, "I'm sorry, but I cannot leave him like that." I was referring to the emotional state of my father. So I went back into my body, but it was a difficult decision to make because that light was incredibly amazing.

When I woke again, I was no longer in my room. I opened my eyes to see two paramedics over me working very hard and very quickly. My first words were, "What the hell are you doing to me? Why are you here?" I looked down to assess myself, and I saw that I had urinated all over myself. Now I was really embarrassed. I was still a bit euphoric and almost felt a little high when I began to apologize for my current state of wetness. There were what looked to me like about thirty people in my living room looking at me. Maybe it was fifteen and I was seeing double. Who knows? Police, fire department, and paramedics. One paramedic said to the other, "He has a very low BP [blood pressure]. It's too low. What do we do?"

I was like, "Guys, please, I am fine. In fact, I feel great. Did you guys see the light? Wasn't it amazing? I'm sorry, I don't know why I'm all wet. Okay, let me go. Did anyone else see that light? Why are you people here again?"

I later found out that there had been a fire in the kitchen of my home, which began when my mother turned on the stove. There had been a gas leak for hours coming from the stove in the kitchen before the fire began, so there really was no way to know how many hours I was inhaling the gas fumes before the fire broke out. The fire was small and contained quickly by my parents before the fire department arrived, but the gas fumes had been rising into my room for who knows how long.

I had been clinically dead. I'm not sure for how long exactly, but that is why I pissed myself. Medically, this is what happens when one dies, apparently, but I didn't know that at the time. Probably a good thing that I didn't.

No one else saw the light. No one else heard the "being." I felt like complete shit from head to toe and started to wonder why the hell I hadn't just stayed in the light. I had no pain there; it was great. I felt I had completely fucked up and made the wrong choice. Why would I choose to come back to this life? To the pain and anguish that it was? Why did I even have a choice or the power to choose? Who is given a choice like that? This is really terrible! I want to go back to the light. I want a do over. Will someone please take me back to the fucking light?

The next year of my life was spent trying to figure out what had happened that day. I began to read about other people's near-death experiences, and many were exactly like mine. Not all of them, but most of them. This is how you can rule out the fakers. When someone tells me they died and woke up, I ask them if they woke up wet. If they say no or "What do you mean?" I know they didn't die; they were hallucinating or making it up. You can't hold in urine when you are dead. I was never lucky enough to find another person who really was there at the light that I could compare notes with. Only others' written accounts. That was very disappointing.

This is where my analytical brain takes over and puts me in my place. "Now let's think about this, Ray." That's how I talk to myself. "You fell in front of a window on what was likely a sunny day. Hence, the white, warm light. And you felt euphoric because you were so frigging high from inhaling gas fumes all night, which also caused hallucinations. See, simple explanation." I accepted this as my truth and told no one what I'd seen for many years. Fear of being ridiculed, fueled by my own lack of belief in an afterlife.

Today is very different, however. Today, I can tell you that death is truly a life-changing experience.

CHAPTER 9:

The Journal

In recent years, I began keeping a journal of these so-called "psychic" occurrences, so I could begin to see and study the things as they happened. I needed to figure out whether these premonitions were real, and the only way I could think of doing so was to write them down or type them and then see if they happened in the future. Basically, the primary purpose of the journal was to figure out if I was sane. I'd also have to figure out who the messages I'd get were for. Rarely, if ever, were they for me. I kept a detailed account of each time I received something—the message itself, who or what it came from, when it came, and the feelings I would have during the incident. All of this information proved to be very useful later when I sought help for myself.

The journal enabled me to recount my experiences with an energy healer and a clairvoyant/medium. At first, they were the only people I would share anything with aside from my girlfriend. I thought the rest of the world would think I was crazy. Hell, even I thought I was crazy!

Each time something happened, I would do my best to quickly write it down or text some of it to myself so I could recall it and then get the entire occurrence in detail in my journal before losing or forgetting any information. This was more difficult than it sounds because I am being hit with something I cannot explain, and I have nothing to compare it to other than my previous experiences, and often there aren't any words that actually describe what is transpiring.

For example, if I tell you that I was "speaking" with a dead person, in actuality, no one is "speaking" at all, but it best describes what is transpiring so you'll understand that we were communicating? There is also no "hearing" or actual "feeling" either. It is just a transmission of information from one energy-based being to another energy-based being. It's strictly telepathic. The primary five senses we have as humans aren't involved. That being said however when I receive the information it may feel to me as though I am hearing, seeing, touching, etc. even though I realize I am not using physical senses.

The paragraph below came from my journal. It was originally entered in the winter of 2018. If I recorded the exact date or month of any given journal entry, then I include that with each entry as we move through the book. The remaining chapters of this book mainly follow my journal entries that were originally recorded as notes. They have been rewritten so you gain the context of the story and in some cases, maintain the privacy of others.

"Jesus Never Speaks" (Journal Entry—Winter, Late 2018)

I know of one divine being. I have been lucky enough to be in his presence a small handful of times. I have since met with other mediums who have told me individually that Jesus is with me. Now, I am not prepared to say whether this is Jesus because I simply do not know, and I do not support or advocate one religion over any other, but here's what I can tell you about him.

Being in his presence is unlike anything else I have ever experienced in the metaphysical world thus far. He has shown up at some really difficult times during my premonitions, some that were very hard to look at, such as a murder or a dangerous situation that I must address or someone will die. I'm talking about the serious shit that I see sometimes. These things can really rattle a person because you now have to figure out what to do with this information before something terrible happens to someone. This causes a significant amount of anxiety, as I am sure you can imagine. I am usually on the verge of a full-blown panic attack, but when he comes, everything else disappears. In an instant, all the negative thoughts and feelings leave my body and mind.

A peaceful calm takes over and, somehow, I just know what I am supposed to do next. He never speaks but does not have to. Just his presence changes everything about me. He is accompanied by a euphoric feeling that goes directly into me. I see everything clearly. I am relaxed. I feel great, and I just seem to "know" what to do next. It is truly amazing.

Aside from these characteristics, there is one more trait that will let you know when you are with him. There is no light behind him. There is always some light present in every one of my visions, but with him, he is the carrier of the light or the director of the light, and therefore, there is very little behind him. It is incredible to see, and I know I am in the presence of a divine celestial being, and I am grateful and honored to be there.

Part II
Seventh Heaven—"Our Lives"

CHAPTER 10:

Boy Meets Girl

I'll never forget how I met Jessica. I was visiting dating sites, and when I considered joining one of them, I put in the preliminary information about myself but withheld my payment. I wasn't sure if I wanted to join or not. The site showed me a few potential "matches" that I might like in the hopes that I would pay to join. One of the profiles of the example matches I was given, instantly caught my attention. Her name was Jessica. I'll never forget the feeling I had the first time I saw her. I had to have her. I had to make her mine. I knew I would love her forever.

I joined the site—which I am fairly certain charges men more than women, by the way. This was not a cheap site. They claimed they could really find a perfect match for anyone. Okay, let's see what you got, website.

Below is the first message I sent through the site to Jessica. It would be the only message I sent through the site. I wasn't interested in anyone else. It had to be her. Just her. I had dated a lot of women, and I was fed up with dating. I wanted Jessica.

Here is our initial correspondence with one another taken from the dating website...

XXXXX.com

Jun 11, 2018 7:45 AM

Hi Jessica,

When I was debating whether to join this particular dating website, the site allowed me to see a few profiles with the intent of persuading me to join. I imagine all sites similar to this one basically do the same thing, but I wanted you to know that it was your profile that actually made me take out my credit card and join. I hope this doesn't apply too much pressure to make you reply. LOL. But I suppose if I don't get one, I may have to request a refund from XXXXX.com and express my dissatisfaction with the website in multiple reviews all over the Internet. So, since it would seem the entire future of my impression of this website hinges directly upon your reply, I do hope to hear from you, and I am betting XXXXX.com as well as my credit card company both feel the same, not to mention the employees of each company, their family members, and various stakeholders, all of whom must be on the edge of their seats right now waiting with great anticipation for your positive response. I hope you find my sarcasm humorous. I look forward to hearing from you. Have a great day!

Sincerely, Ray.

June 11, 2018 5.53 PM

Lolol!!! This is a hysterical response!! I haven't even looked at your profile yet. I just read this & laughed.... Who are you & where do you live?!!

June 11, 2018 10:02 PM

I just read your profile. I love it! I like your sense of humor & your values....

Jessica

That is how it all started. Things would never be the same after that for either of us.

Jessica is such a critical part of this story. It was when I originally agreed to have my first spiritual clearing that she purchased for me as a gift that the floodgates opened into my brain with regard to the metaphysical world and the various paranormal instances that came soon thereafter.

She and I always knew there was just something about our relationship that made it feel different from any other. Almost like we knew each other before we met, that type of feeling—many déjà vu moments, if you will.

After a bit of dating and following one of our long conversations, Jessica told me she thought I needed more spirituality in my life. I couldn't argue that point. She was right. I had none. I didn't know what my beliefs were at all. I was trying to decipher them myself just prior to the time we met. Oh, the irony! A few months later, she bought me a spiritual clearing to be performed by an energy healer she knew. It was a birthday present. I feigned slight excitement. I had no idea what this was at that time, but I remember thinking, this girl is super-hot and I'll just do whatever she says.

Shortly after that, Jessica scheduled my spiritual clearing.

CHAPTER 11:
Rapture of Romance

Our relationship has blossomed into a beautiful love affair right out of a romance novel. We text each other multiple times per day just to say "I love you." I send her gifts or flowers so they are waiting there when she gets home. I pride myself on the fact that I have never let Jessica open a door for herself in the history of our relationship. Chivalry is not dead, I assure you. I pull out her chair at the restaurant, help her on with her coat, and I will absolutely physically and/or psychologically destroy anything that even thinks about doing her harm without hesitation or fear of my own potential negative consequences.

I remember that in the second month we were dating, I had to have surgery. It wasn't life threatening for me, but it was still surgery. She sat by my bedside until I left that hospital. I'll never forget that. I trust her, and I assure you, I trust no one. She understands what it means to be loyal, and where I come from, there is no other attribute more important than that.

This is not to say that we, just like all couples, have never had our ups and downs. We have, but the downs are not something we ever allow to keep us down. We are able to talk through our differences. We are able to hear the other person's side of things. We are able to work through these disagreements by reminding ourselves of the love we have for each other. And if all else fails, we will just have crazy sex until we are both tired and end up laughing about whatever the hell we were fighting over in the first place. Try this yourself; it works. A few orgasms and the whole world's simply perfect again.

On a more intimate level, I simply cannot get enough of her. If we are alone (which isn't easy with both of us having kids), within minutes I am tearing at her clothes while passionately kissing her, making her feel like the most desirable woman in the world—and that is very easy to do because that's exactly what she is.

I love doing even the simplest things with her. Sometimes as simple as cooking, doing yoga, working out, taking a shower, walking in a park, or hiking. Just sitting somewhere with a nice atmosphere and having coffee, hearing about her day, staring at her, listening to her voice, or even just sleeping with her head on my chest.

Of course, I absolutely love driving her crazy with anticipation—anticipation of my love and passion for her.

I asked Jessica what I should put in this chapter of the book about us, and she said without hesitation, "Oh my God, the things you say to me, the things you do for me…"

"Oh, I get it now. Careful what you wish for, babe."

So, I made a list. Keep in mind that this list is only from *my* perspective of what I do for her and say to her. Perhaps her list would be a bit different.

Twenty ways to keep her crazy in love with you…

1. Listen to her. Every fucking word! Really listen. Women say eight words to a man's one. Get used to it.

2. Always have her back whether she's right or wrong, especially in public. If she bumped into someone, what the fuck was that someone doing there in the first place? Get the idea?

3. Men drive on dates or use a car service, and for God's sake, open the door for her, not just the lock.

4. Never let her carry anything other than her purse. Don't offer to take that. That is part of her outfit, dummy.

5. Go to fancy places where she can get dressed up sometimes. She wants you to stare at her.

6. Stare at her!

7. Go to places where it is acceptable for her to wear a little less clothing—the beach, the gym, etc.

8. Stare at her!

9. Please, never let her pay the bill on a date. What's more, never split the bill. I don't care if you have been married for twenty years to a feminist, men pay the damn bill.

10. Experience things with her that she likes to do. Take her to a spa together. Don't just give her a gift card. Go with her for the actual experience.

11. Get creative with sex. Cook at home together, naked or just in an apron is pretty hot. Play with the utensils that aren't sharp. I think that goes without saying, but who knows?

12. Get out of the house to have sex. Find a hotel with a fireplace, hot tub, or both.

13. Text her all day the dirty things you want to do to her later, tomorrow, this weekend, or whenever the next "sex play time" is. Call, text, email, etc.

14. Have sex everywhere, not just in a bed or a house. Cars, yards, gazebos, and bathrooms are all great too.

15. Read a book about the vagina. There is *so* much you can do with it. Most women can have several different kinds of orgasms. Learn them.

16. Explore fetishes, fantasies, and toys. Let her talk about sex. Her likes and dislikes. Don't be a dick about it. Take care of her needs first, and you will be a very happy man, I promise you.

17. Do not ask her if she "feels like" having sex tonight. If you ask, you've already killed the mood. Just be a fucking man, please. If she really doesn't want to, she will *really* let you know.

18. Cuddle the shit out of her after sex. Why? Don't you want her to remember who made her feel that way? Every time she just smells you, she will think of that amazing orgasm you gave her.

19. You are only as good as your last orgasm—the one you gave, not the one you had.

20. Tell her how much you love her and why. Yes, why! Try to think of new ways to say this often. Since many reasons may be repetitive, try to make the delivery unique each time. Every day!

Oh, I can hear the women readers chuckling already: "How will I get my husband to read this? 'Honey, I have a great book about a clairvoyant atheist. You simply must read it!'"

The way Jessica makes me feel, I look forward to these things and more. It's always a pleasure. It's never a chore. I want to be her first thought in the morning and her last thought at night, with her head on my chest saying, I love you, goodnight.

She is my best friend, my person. I love you, Jessica!

CHAPTER 12:

Jessica and John

Jessica and I fell in love with each other almost immediately. I had so much respect and admiration for her. I knew early on we were going to be great together. A few months into our relationship, she and I took our first vacation together to Aruba. Jessica had friends who were getting married there, and I was her plus one.

Aruba was beautiful, and the wedding we attended just made it all the more romantic. One night while she and I were alone at dinner, she began to confide in me a few personal details about her life. I guess we were at that point of full disclosure in a relationship: it's time to see if this person is really right for me and vice versa.

Jessica began to share with me in detail the events surrounding her father's death and how it affected her. He'd had an unexpected fatal heart attack at only fifty years of age. Jessica and her dad, John, had been extremely close. Whenever she spoke about him, you could see how much love and admiration she had for him. She would smile from ear to ear and tell me about the things they used to do together and their shared interests. Jessica was an athlete, and her father loved sports and never missed one of her games—at home or on the road; he was always present. He was so proud of her, and she always felt his love, even after his death.

John had a thriving construction business and built many of the homes and buildings in the area where she grew up. Even today, if we drive past a particular building, she will say, "My dad built that." She was, and still is, very proud of him. The people of the neighborhood also loved John, and his wife, Joanna. They would open their doors to all of their friends every Christmas Eve. Everyone was welcome and everyone came. Jessica's friends all remember and tell me stories of this, and of John being a larger-than-life presence and amazing dad, to this day.

Jessica went on to tell me that since the day her father died, she just knew his presence was always around her. Smaller and larger signals were sent from him to her. This began on the day he died. That night, Jessica woke up and was physically ill—not a cold or anything she can describe as a sickness, just an overall feeling of awfulness. She called out of work sick that morning, and she later found out that he had passed during the night. She had multiple visits from him in those first few days, telling her things that she needed to pass along immediately. The first night, Jessica could barely sleep, but at one point, she was startled and saw a vision of a light under a door. She wanted to open the door but couldn't. She tried over and over again to open the door because she just somehow "knew" her dad was on the other side, but there was no door handle to open it with. Finally, John reached through the door and hugged her and said, "It's alright, I am here. We are just in different rooms."

When discussing it, Jessica explained that she could clearly tell the difference between a visit from her dad and a dream, as I now can understand.

Another major thing over the years was the time of day, 11:11 or 1:11. Quite often when a message would come in some form or something ironic transpired in her life, she would check the time and it was always 11:11 or 1:11. I have witnessed this myself with her many times.

There were many other paranormal experiences between her and her dad. While they were both living, she would pick up the phone to call him, but the phone would be dead because he would already be on the line calling her at the exact same time. Back in the days on the old-fashioned landline telephones, this was possible because there was a delay in the first ring of the phone.

Jessica was grief stricken after her father's death. While she continued to have these visits and signs, she desperately missed him. She told me a story of how she finally had the courage to meet with a medium to contact her dad ten years after he had died. She explained that she had waited so long because she was afraid that this, or any medium, would not validate all the experiences she knew she had been having with him. The medium's first name was Joe. We will call him Medium Joe. He was and still is a well-known, highly regarded medium and is quite difficult to get a session with. You will hear more about Medium Joe later in this book when I finally meet with him. When Jessica talks about this experience, she describes it as the day that changed her life because she was no longer grieving and no longer depressed; it was the most amazing thing that ever happened to her.

Medium Joe was able to make contact with her dad John, instantly. Her dad was a powerful man in life and in death. He channeled himself into Medium Joe's body like a bull in a china shop, at one point becoming so overwhelming that Medium Joe, a highly accomplished and extremely experienced medium, began to cry. He apologized to Jessica and stated that rarely had he ever felt this kind of love, intensity, and desperation to talk to one's daughter as he was having at that moment. In fact, her dad would not stay to the side (as is proper spiritual etiquette) but insisted on seeing Jessica full on face forward, so he took over and sat in Medium Joe's chair, which was quite an intense experience for all three of them. Needless to say, Medium Joe and Jessica had an hour and a half of tears, laughs, and just full on wonderment; he said things to her that only her father had said or would've known, described in detail many aspects of their lives and experiences they had, and at one point, even embodied some of her dad's mannerisms and facial expressions. To this day, Jessica speaks of this experience with tears in her eyes and a huge smile on her face.

Jessica says that this singular experience changed her life. This medium gave her the closure she desperately needed and confirmed that her dad was always there looking out for her from beyond this world. Medium Joe also drew a picture of her dad, which, according to Jessica, was spot on and amazing. I hadn't seen it at this point, but her dad was wearing the shirt he had worn on Christmas Eve just before he died. The last known photograph ever taken of her dad was on that night, and it was taken with

Jessica by his side. This picture and the shirt he wore that day will become an important part of my story later on.

There were a few other things that the medium told her during that visit. One was that she was going to have twins; he drew two pink roses, and Jessica has twin girls. He also said that someone else in her family was pregnant at the time (it was her sister but no one knew that yet), and lastly, there would be a person in her life, with the letter "R," who would be of much significance to her. That's me!

Back in Aruba, I listened intently to Jessica's stories of mediumship, the different ways she would make contact with her father, and all of her dad's messages from beyond, and it just broke my heart. I felt so sorry for this poor girl who actually thought her dad was out there looking after her. Remember, at this point, I did not believe in anything, let alone mediums or psychic abilities, but I didn't share this with her. Who was I to take that away from her? If she believed it was real, so be it. I loved her, and I was fine with that.

CHAPTER 13:

The Transformation of an Atheist

Our relationship is like no other. If you have any doubt about that statement, you'll soon see what I mean. Jessica has always had a strong connection with things not of this world. As you know, she believes in mediums, psychic abilities, and the afterlife. She also practices yoga and transcendental meditation and believes in universal energy. At that time, I wasn't sure what I believed, although she was certainly convincing, and I enjoyed hearing about the many "coincidences" and messages that occurred between Jessica and her dad.

When Jessica and I were about to go to bed one night, we began discussing our beliefs, but when she asked me what my beliefs were, I had trouble answering; I really didn't know. I explained to her that while this was something I had wanted to explore, it had always taken a back seat to work and raising my kids.

She said, "Well, maybe meeting me will make you want to explore that and perhaps figure out what your beliefs are. Even if they are different from mine, shouldn't you at least find out?"

As usual, I agreed that she had a very good point. This really was something I'd had on my to-do list, but because I thought it had very little significance or importance at this point in my life, I just kept putting it off. Also, hearing the stories of her, her dad, and Joe the medium, had definitely piqued my curiosity. I still didn't believe, but I thought it would be worth figuring out what I did believe in. Even if it was nothing at all, I should confirm it.

The next week, Jessica told me she had purchased a spiritual clearing for me for my birthday. I had no idea what that was and later that night I admittedly had to look it up. I will go into more detail later in this book about the process, but suffice to say it is done by an energy healer who, with the help of her energy and connection with the universe, "clears" a path between you and the spiritual universe for energy to flow freely and naturally.

I said, "That's wonderful, babe. Thank you. So, will we be having cake?"

She could tell I wasn't that enthused. I didn't have any understanding of what exactly was about to happen, but I think somehow she did. She has a bit of psychic ability herself, but she chose not to reveal this to me at the time.

My clearing was performed by a friend of Jessica named Nicole. She is an amazing energy healer who lives near us. You will read more about her later in this book, as she was one of the catalysts of the paranormal experiences that were to follow.

I remember some of the things Nicole told me during the first few times she and I met, one in particular stands out more than any other. She had asked me if I was interested in astronomy. I told her that as a child, it was one of my favorite subjects at school. For my science project, I chose to recreate the solar system. I absolutely loved learning about the universe, and I received an A+ on that class project. I asked her why she asked that question and how it pertained to me now.

She responded, "I am not sure why exactly, but you must return to reading and learning about astronomy."

So, I took her advice, and I returned to reading and learning about astronomy. It was doing that research that helped me to discover the science behind my experiences. Remember that I do not believe anything unless it can be backed up by science. The third part of this book evolved from accepting that advice from Nicole.

Nicole made two other very profound statements in one of our follow-up emails that also make much more sense to me now:

> Message from the Masters: "The bonfire within is just a spark now. Work with this spark to ignite the creation that lies ahead. Ask for guidance and lean into that spark. The path will be illuminated

for you. Trust, see, live. The beauty will unfold. There is magic surrounding; wait and it will all be revealed to you."

Suggestions: Your session was focused mostly on honoring the process of transformation. During your affirmation work, try to notice something that came up the previous day surrounding the topic of change and attempt to extract something positive from that recognition. With practice, you can honor the flow around you, allowing the flow within to be something you honor as well. Also, practice aligning your creations with others. Perhaps bringing compassion and tolerance to this will aid your shift to work in alignment so that you may create, in an open-minded way, with clear motivation and dedication.

These initial conversations with Nicole were at the very beginning of my journey. I had no idea who or what my masters were, and I certainly had no idea of the complete transformation I was about to undergo in the next year. As you read this book to the end of my story, remember that Nicole told us this in the very beginning.

Let us return to my clearing and what comes thereafter.

The clearing was done, and I didn't need to be present for it, but I knew it was completed, first, because I knew when it was going to be done and by whom it would be done, and second, because I actually felt differently afterward, physically and emotionally different. I wasn't prepared to say for better or for worse at that point just yet—just different. It was, however, as if I had given the universe and all the energies within it permission to enter through me. The clearing would later prove to be a life-changing event for me.

A few days after the clearing, I began to have little eight-second-long daydreams. There were usually a couple of people in them that I did not recognize, and there would be a message in the form of one or two sentences that meant very little to me. I casually told myself that I needed to drink less coffee and went on with my life.

However, the same daydream returned another day. Every time I allowed my mind a moment to rest, the daydream returned. Jessica was in it, and there was a man as well. I did not know who he was, but he kept saying the same line over and over to me: "I fucked up; I made a mistake. You can help her. I can't."

I saw Jessica in the daydream with a look of horror on her face. She was looking at something that I could not see. I did not know the man at all. He resembled no one remotely familiar to me. The daydream continued to return—when I was in the shower, when I was driving, when I took a break at work, and at any moment I allowed my mind to not focus on anything in particular. As soon as my mind was idle, it would come back.

Along with the daydream came these vibrations inside my body. They began around my knees and continued up into the midsection of my abdomen. The vibrations were very low. Low in the feeling and low down in my body. They were quite disruptive to the point that it was beginning to really piss me off.

By day three, I could not function as a normal human being because I was consumed with these deep, low, annoying vibrations and this damn daydream that played itself over and over in my mind.

Who was this man? Why was this happening to me? What the fuck was going on? Was I crazy? There it was again: "I fucked up; I made a mistake. You can help her. I can't."

"Help her do what already?" I screamed in my mind. At least, I think it was in my mind, but who knows at this point?

Should I tell Jessica I keep seeing this? She was a doctor of psychology; she would think I was fucking nuts and dump me. At no point did I think this was a real message because, remember, I didn't believe in that shit. How will I tell Jessica? What will I say?

By this time, I was actually taking medication to calm down. This feeling inside me was so bad that I couldn't concentrate, I couldn't work, and I couldn't even drive properly. I had an overwhelming desire to share this "dream" with Jessica, but I didn't have any idea why.

At the end of day three before nightfall, I talked to Jessica and told her I kept having the same dream while I was sleeping. I told her I'd had it three nights in a row. I couldn't tell her I "saw" it all day long, as I felt sure she would break up with me thinking I was a fucking crazy person.

I said something like, "I need to tell you about a recurring dream I have had for the last three nights."

"Okay," she said.

"In this recurring dream, I see a man getting up either out of a chair or up off the floor. I cannot tell which because I can only see him from the shoulders up. His back is toward me, but he turns to one side and says, 'I fucked up; I made a mistake. You can help her. I can't.' The man has facial hair. His shirt or jacket reminds me of an older style of clothes from the 1980s or 1990s."

"You are in this scene as well, standing to my left with a look of horror on your face. You are looking over my left shoulder at something that I cannot see. I can only see your face."

"The dream replays over and over and over again non-stop. The same eight seconds when he gets up, turns his head to me, and says, 'I fucked up; I made a mistake. You can help her. I can't.'"

She said, "Do you think it is my dad?"

I said, "Absolutely not" with confidence. "I have seen the picture of your dad in your bedroom, and this guy I saw did not resemble that picture at all. The guy I saw in the dream had a full beard and mustache and was a bit heavier than your dad."

"Hold on," she said.

After two minutes, she texted me a picture of a man with a beard and a mustache and asked, "Is it him?"

I said, "Holy shit! That is the guy in the scene! Do you know him?" I dropped my phone on the floor, but quickly picked it up and texted back, "Who is that?"

"That is my dad, silly. In the picture on my dresser, he was clean shaven, and he had lost some weight."

I was shocked to say the least, but Jessica said he had always sent her messages. That is when I admitted to her that it wasn't exactly a dream but more of a daytime vision that had been haunting me for three days.

Jessica said to me, "Maybe you're a psychic medium and just don't know it." She began to laugh at me.

"That is not the least bit funny, Jessica. Don't even say that kidding around, please. I would never want to bear that burden."

I began to get more regular "messages" after delivering that one to Jessica, and I began writing them down to remember them. Is it possible that I do actually have this ability and Jessica's dad is speaking to me? This is absolutely insane, I thought. Don't they know that I don't believe they exist? Why in the world would they choose an atheist to communicate with?

The gates between the two worlds were open now, and I started getting messages every day. More of these same types of messages came through. The similar eight-second loop type that continuously played over and over again. Why did Jessica's dad keep returning to talk to me? What the hell did he want with me?

Was it possible that John had found me, a person who could communicate with both him and the living? And I happened to be his daughter's boyfriend. He must have been fucking thrilled. According to Jessica, he was always trying to connect with her through various means with signals and signs, but now he had me, he was never going to leave me alone!

Remember the story of when Jessica's dad came through Medium Joe and he said that her dad was like a bull in a china shop? I completely understood that now. Jessica's dad had messages to get through, and he'd just found a guy close enough to his daughter to get them through, literally.

I shared some of the newer messages with Jessica, and she always seemed to know the people in these "daydreams." She could also tell me with accuracy who the messages were for. This was getting really crazy now, but I needed to know whether this was real or whether I was headed to the nut house.

Jessica suggested we go and see a very well known, accomplished, psychic medium we will call Medium Bonnie, who was coming to our area soon. Jessica had a phone session scheduled with her in the next few days and knew that she was coming to our area in the next couple of weeks or so. "You can meet with her and get your answers," she said to me.

Medium Bonnie requested a picture of me from Jessica during their telephone conversation. She explained to Jessica that it is rather unusual for men to have these abilities and not to get too excited about the possibilities of me having such. Even if they have some ability, getting men to use them and perfect them is extremely rare.

I was told later that Medium Bonnie said something like this after seeing my picture: "Ah... Jessica? Ray is the real deal! Please bring him in!"

Jessica knew this was not necessarily the answer I wanted to hear. I most certainly didn't want it to be real. I just wanted to hear, "You're all right, and you are not crazy," and be sent on my way. I had too much going on in my life for this—not to mention that communicating with energies from other realms is super exhausting and extremely uncomfortable! It was really unpleasant for me at this point. Also, what would people think of me? What would they want from me? Would I lose my job, my career? What could I really do to help anyone, anyway? Needless to say, I was not sure at this point whether I was going to actually go through with meeting Medium Bonnie.

Nevertheless, Jessica booked two sessions for us with the medium and I reluctantly agreed to go. Please don't let this be real, I thought.

But then again, if it isn't real, then I *am* frigging nuts and then what would I do?

Jessica's dad continues to be an integral part of this story. He had unfinished business here on Earth, and he wanted me to get these things done for him. Remember I said he is like a bull in a china shop when he visits? He's a powerhouse in life and in death. He was used to getting what he wants, and the simple fact that he's dead wasn't going to deter him one bit. Once he figured out that I could "hear" and "see" him, it was on. He could shake my insides like a tree branch in a hurricane if he wanted to.

Can you imagine, of all the dead people out there who wished to make contact with me, mine had to be my potential future father-in-law?

Go ahead; you can laugh. I did. Eventually. Not for a long while, but eventually I did.

CHAPTER 14:

Meeting the Real Deal

Before discussing my phenomenon with Medium Bonnie (who later became my first teacher), I did not do any research. I had never read a book on this topic and never spoke of having any abilities with anyone but Jessica. If I was going to discuss this with a medium who is known to be the real deal, I did not want to have any preconceived notions that would alter my memory of my personal experiences. In other words, I wanted to find out if this was real by comparing my exact experiences to other psychic mediums and their experiences to see if we all saw and felt the same things the same way.

This is also what I did with my near-death experience. After writing mine down, I began doing as much research as I could find on the topic to see if all of us who experienced a near-death event saw the same thing and felt the same thing. Many of us did, almost precisely.

It had been about six months since the spiritual clearing. I had my journal of my personal experiences and premonitions with me, so I could take them to Medium Bonnie for validation. I was admittedly still quite skeptical of my own abilities and their authentication, but I was now open to the idea that others might have them. I had never been to visit a medium, psychic, or anything like that, and I didn't know what to expect. I was feeling a bit lost and confused, which is the worst feeling for someone like me. I am admittedly a bit of a control freak, and this "thing" of mine was certainly not within my control at this point. It was our first meeting, and it sort of went like this.

Medium Bonnie had been told by Jessica that she would set up a face-to-face meeting for her to meet me. Up until this point, only Jessica knew of my so-called "abilities."

Medium Bonnie also told Jessica in that same conversation that she is my oracle and I am Jessica's warrior. "You continually charge and recharge him," she said. During Jessica's session, she had brought up a recent disagreement we had been having, and Medium Bonnie stopped her, telling Jessica that "it would be very dangerous for you and Ray to break up."

"Dangerous?" Jessica asked.

Medium Bonnie continued that we must give this relationship at least six more months before we decide to do anything. Jessica explained that we were not planning on breaking up, but Medium Bonnie, who was usually lighthearted and somewhat casual in the way she delivered her messages, stopped her and stated, "At least six months, you have to trust me."

Jessica convinced me to go meet Medium Bonnie by explaining if I didn't go, I would never find out the truth about myself, and that she was rarely in our part of the country and, therefore, if I did not meet her now, I might not be able to for quite some time.

Jessica and I arrived at the house where the medium was staying and working out of. I went in to see her first. If I'd have gone second, I might have backed out. I was so nervous. I went into her office.

"Hi, my name is Ray."

"Nice to meet you, Ray. I am Bonnie."

She stopped and said nothing for about two full seconds, which seemed like hours. Her eyes began to blink, and she suddenly got a huge burst of energy and said, "Oh! You are *that* Ray! How can I help you today, Ray?"

Holy shit! I am *that* Ray! Get me out of here, please!

I was so nervous. Up until now, I hadn't told anyone anything about this. Was she going to laugh me out of her office, or worse, what would I do if it was real? I took a breath and said, "I think I am losing my mind."

"What makes you say that?" she asked.

"Help Her" (Journal Entry—Summer, 2019)

I began to tell her about one of my premonitions. This first one I told her about was the one involving Jessica's dad. Below is the conversation as I remember it.

"In my mind, I am in front of a movie screen. I see a man getting up either out of a chair or up off the floor. I cannot tell which because I can only see parts of the body, never an entire body. I can see him from the shoulders up. His back is toward me, but he turns to one side and says, 'I fucked up; I made a mistake. You can help her. I can't.' The man has facial hair, quite a bit of it. His shirt or jacket reminds me of an older style of clothes from the eighties or nineties. Jessica is in this scene standing to my left with a look of horror on her face. She is looking at something that I cannot see. I can only see her face. The scene replays over and over and over again nonstop—the same eight seconds, where he gets up, turns his head to me, and says, 'I fucked up; I made a mistake. You can help her. I can't.'"

Medium Bonnie explained that the "movie screen" is how we (clairvoyants and mediums) get those types of messages and that we rarely get to see a whole body. We get parts of the body and then have to figure it out. She asked if the picture was fragmented, and I said "yes," and that it looked like it was in mostly black and white with just a touch of color.

"That is it, Ray. That is exactly right." She confirmed that it was absolutely necessary to tell Jessica or whomever is in the scene what I saw. "What happened after you told Jessica?" she asked.

"It completely went away," I said.

"Exactly," she said. "So this would have not followed you around for three days disrupting your life had you just told Jessica of her dad's message upon receiving it the first time."

That is easier said than done. For starters, the more times I see the movie, the clearer it is and the clearer the message becomes. Some fragments didn't come into the picture until the tenth or twentieth time I viewed it.

She told me that it was okay, and the process would improve over time. Just let it out and add to it later so that it doesn't drive you crazy.

This was the first time I thought this just might be real.

"Silly Shoes" (Journal Entry—Summer, 2019)

I went on to share another experience with Medium Bonnie.

In this one, Jessica was out to dinner with a woman we will call Maria. I was at home flipping through the television looking for something to watch, and it was taking me a while to find anything of interest. For a brief moment, I began to think about Jessica's dad and the last experience I had with him, but then something else happened.

There was the movie screen again. There was just one man in the front wearing all white and behind him were black hats. The black hats were on men's heads, but they didn't really look entirely like men. They were doing something sneaky behind this man's back with money in their hands. He said to me, "I regret everything. These people came after me for the money." He had much love for this woman he was speaking to, I knew that, and furthermore, he felt terrible about whatever happened to the money. He said one more thing to me before he left: "Remember the silly shoes."

At the time, this completely confused me, but I took it to Jessica and she said, "I think the message is from Maria's husband, the lady I had dinner with last night."

I said, "That can't be right. He isn't dead, is he?"

She said, "Oh yes, he is."

I was dumbfounded. I begged Jessica, "If you're going to tell Maria, please don't tell her it is from me. I don't want anyone to know I can do this, please."

"Fine. I'll say I was on the phone with my medium. That way, I am not really lying to her. You are my medium."

"Oh, one more thing," I added. "This man said, 'Remember the silly shoes.' If that means something to her, I'll believe this is real. He gave me that as he was leaving, so to speak."

The next day, Jessica reported back. She said Maria told her about an occurrence on their first date when he showed up with the most ridiculous shoes she had ever seen. It was a running joke throughout their entire marriage. She was so thankful and appreciative of receiving the entire message from her dead husband. It gave her some closure that she needed. She needed to know that he didn't mean to leave her in a bad financial way, and he also wanted her to know how much he loved her. I felt good about that, but I still didn't want anyone to know the message came from me.

Medium Bonnie said the dead will often make a statement that is off the wall, like the mention of the silly shoes to prove to their loved one that the message is real.

Two for two. It was looking really real now!

"Heed Advice" (Journal Entry—Summer, 2019)

I also told Medium Bonnie about the time I had a similar movie experience with a woman sitting in her chair in her office. It looked like a typical psychologist's office with a chair for the doctor (her) and a couch for the patients. Jessica was the patient, which was quite odd because Jessica is a doctor of psychology. I could only see the other woman from the waist down. She had a very attractive figure and was wearing a skirt and heels. She was recently single and looking for a man. She'd had a terrible break-up that really affected her emotionally, to the point that it was interfering with her career. The message was for Jessica to take her relationship advice with a grain of salt due to the terrible break-up she'd had.

I brought this to Jessica because I figured this one was just so off the wall. It didn't make sense to me. I gave her the message, and she immediately knew exactly who it was. The break-up was very bad, and this poor woman was so distraught, she had to shut down her practice temporarily to get over this traumatic event. The physical description of the woman was correct as well. The thing about this one was that both parties in the scene were very much alive. So, who sent this one to me, and why?

Medium Bonnie explained that you can absolutely have premonitions about the living. This is just another type of psychic ability. She went on to tell me I had multiple abilities happening all at once, which was extremely rare for men.

She asked me if I'd ever heard of a "word drop." This is when you hear one word out of nowhere for no apparent reason. I had a eureka moment. Aha! Is that what it is? A word drop? I used to have those a lot when I lived in my old apartment. They drove me crazy. I used to look under the bed, in the closets, and in the showers with a baseball bat in my hand thinking, Who the fuck is in my house?

Three for three, and a hundred percent validation. Holy crap, now what?

For the remainder of our time together, we just chit-chatted about the things that would annoy or get under the skin of any psychic. I asked her, what was the one question she hated getting the most. At the same time, we both answered and said aloud "How do you know that? Hahahaha!"

I was like, "Oh my God! My entire life, I have hated that question. I have no frigging idea how I know anything."

She said, "Me too!" And we laughed a lot for the rest of our time together.

When it was time for me to go, I asked Medium Bonnie for a business card to keep in touch, but she said, "I don't have anymore, but I have a website and a book. I'm easy to find." I was disappointed. I thought she didn't really want to ever see me again.

Jessica went in to see Medium Bonnie after me, and the first thing she said to Jessica was, "I don't take on new students any longer, but I am going to teach Ray!"

In the car later, after both of our sessions were over, Jessica said, "So when do you start working with Medium Bonnie?"

"What do you mean?"

"She is taking you on as a student," Jessica replied.

"That never came up in our conversation. Are you sure?"

"Of course, I am sure," Jessica said.

"She didn't even seem to want to give me her contact information," I replied. Jessica laughed out loud as if our new psychic friend knew something I didn't. Then again, I thought, of course she does!

"Slow Down, Just Breathe" (Journal Entry—Summer, 2019)

It wasn't long after our first meeting that I reached out to my new medium teacher to begin learning everything she was willing to share with me. We would mostly speak by telephone for about an hour each time since Medium Bonnie traveled quite a bit. I continued to keep my journal of experiences so I could go over them with her in our sessions. Essentially, I would explain to her each phenomenon as they occurred, and she would explain to me what they were, how to amplify them, and how to decode them.

She also taught me how to meditate in such a way that would make it easier for me to be in the state of mind of being ready, willing, and able to receive messages clearly. Before I could meditate properly, these messages would pop up randomly in my mind and be quite disruptive to my everyday life. For example, do you know that feeling when you just sort of drift off somewhere with your mind? You may have experienced this yourself in school when sitting through a lecture, and then the teacher stops the lecture and asks you a question. You can't answer because you were daydreaming and didn't hear the teacher speaking to you in the first place. That happens to me often to this day. When it happens to me, though, I can go into an altered state of mind, and vivid messages can sometimes come through.

I got many of my messages during these times, typically when I was doing something mundane that I could do without thinking, such as brushing my teeth or showering. Then, there are times they appear that can be detrimental, such as when I'm driving a car. It also happens when I take a break from reading the computer screen. It's even happened in a very important business meeting where I was supposed to be listening to someone speaking to me, and at other times when I was the one speaking but I was saying something that was very well rehearsed. These are the times I had to gain control of. Learning to meditate is what primarily gave me the ability to control these events and not have them control me.

This ancient practice of drifting off into a daydream to retrieve messages was referred to as scrying, which is when I believe the crystal ball first came into use. It was believed, and was probably true, that looking at or into a shiny object would help oneself enter this altered state of mind more easily and quickly.

There isn't one specific way to meditate. In fact, it is more about finding which way works for you as an individual. The goal of meditation in any case is the same: to reach a higher level of consciousness. We want to connect with the universal collective consciousness. How we each get there can vary. I suggest learning many techniques to develop your own method.

Medium Bonnie and I went through different methods, but it was a combination of hers, Jessica's, and my own suggestions that eventually clicked for me. I will share with you my method, but don't get disappointed if mine doesn't work for you. You'll have to practice regularly to find your own path. If it were easy, everyone would do it. I compare it to going to the gym and working out daily. Each day gets you somewhat closer to your goal of getting yourself in better shape. It doesn't happen overnight. However, you may surprise yourself and you may achieve your goal sooner rather than later.

When I first began to meditate, I tried to be in a quiet, peaceful space. Eventually, this won't matter as much. You do not have to sit in any particular fashion, but there are a few methods I follow. I prefer to keep my palms up to receive. This may do absolutely nothing, but I like it. In the beginning, you can be comfortable, but eventually you may want to deliberately make yourself a little more uncomfortable. You see, this is mind over matter. You should eventually not be able to feel your body, and then it won't actually matter if you began comfortably or not.

Close your eyes, palms up, sit upright, and do not move a muscle under any circumstances. Your nose or face may itch when you begin, but this is normal. This is your brain (not your mind) trying to fuck with you. It is completely unnatural for the body not to move. Therefore, the brain will do things to try to make sure you do move. Overpower your brain with your mind and don't fucking move.

If you are like me, you probably have many thoughts racing through your mind when you begin. It's fine for now. If you need to spend a few minutes with those thoughts, it is okay to do so. Eventually, they will fade away. During these moments, you may breathe normally. Eventually, your breathing will slow down a bit naturally. If you like, you may take a few deep breaths in the very beginning. This is just a personal preference. Let's begin.

Before beginning the breathing exercises listed below or any exercises please be sure to consult with your health care provider.

Start by inhaling a full deep breath, the maximum amount of air you can take in slowly, and once your lungs are full, hold it for five seconds. Then, exhale all the air from your lungs slowly but comfortably, and when you have no air remaining, again count five seconds. Breathe in slowly and as deeply as possible and hold it again for five seconds before exhaling slowly. Once again, when your lungs are completely emptied, count five seconds. You should repeat this inhale and exhale technique at least five times. The objective is to slow your natural state of breathing all the way down to being still and to almost not breathing at all. If five times isn't enough, do another couple of times.

Here is exactly what I do from this point. You may use this or change anything you wish. There is no right or wrong here.

I focus on my breath. I imagine my breath as the color blue. I inhale blue and I exhale blue. Each time I exhale the color blue, a cloud of my blue breath gets larger and larger. I continue to breathe blue, and I continue to make a bigger blue cloud of breath in front of me until that cloud is all I can see. If my mind begins to wander, I go back to my blue breath, creating a blue cloud that's ever increasing in size. I am purposely saying blue a lot because that is also what I am saying in my mind when I do this.

Eventually, my mind sees only the blue cloud. I no longer feel my body, and the blue cloud approaches the veil that separates our worlds. This could take minutes or it may take hours to reach this point. Everyone is different, and practice makes it much easier. At this point, I usually see darkness beyond the cloud. I move across the cloud to the end of the line where the blue and black meet, and I know I am about to cross over. Once I move completely into the black, I know I've crossed and I open my eyes. Not my real eyes. My mind's eye. I then begin to look around. I have no idea who or what will be there. It is here where I have met my guides and seen many other visions you'll soon read about in this book.

It is important to note that some mediums believe that guides and masters are actually deceased folks who you have known or who know you and wish to help you, but they choose not to reveal their identity to you. They are not necessarily assigned to you to help you, but we know they exist. They do not appear in human form.

Since I have learned to meditate well, I've been able to better control the "drifting off" type of messages. I can still have them and I do have them, but they aren't as disruptive. I can turn some of them off quickly and return to what I was doing if I choose to. I can then go back to get them later through meditating on my terms when I am ready.

I have several different types of meditations now that are used for different purposes. I have one for manifestation, I have one to relieve pain, both physical and emotional. I have another that simply puts me into a very positive, happy place. I call it mindful meditation. Guided meditation can be quite beneficial as well if you are just beginning this journey or simply need the extra help to stay focused.

Exploring meditation is one of the greatest things I have ever done for myself. I speak about meditation often these days to people I meet with. Those who say they meditate, will follow that up with, but I have difficulty finding the time. You don't need much time. You can meditate for five minutes at one sitting if that is all the time you have. Meditation doesn't have to be an hour long. There are no rules with meditation. Five minutes at a time is much better than not doing it at all. Learn to meditate. It will change your life.

"Good Vibrations" (Journal Entry—Winter, Early 2020)

Later in this book, you will read the science behind each method I practice and use. I do not believe in any magic, hocus pocus shit, and I certainly have absolutely no blind faith in anything or anyone. Prove it to me scientifically, or I am not buying it. That being the case, what is the scientific reason for meditation? What does it do? What is its purpose, and what are we trying to achieve? I will try to answer these questions by combining my own personal theories with those of some of the smartest humans of all time.

Some people enjoy watching television or reading books that are entertaining in some way, as do I. However, most often I would prefer to learn about someone or something when I am reading or watching a show. So, while some will curl up with a nice romance novel or a mystery, I prefer a book about a famous scientist or physicist and their discoveries, or a nice documentary on quantum physics. As you already know, I also enjoy astronomy. In this particular case, I will reference my learning about Nikola Tesla. The famous inventor that always seems to escape our history books for some reason. I suppose that reason is because he never really achieved any great wealth from his discoveries. Meanwhile, he may just be the most important inventor to ever walk this Earth. I highly recommend reading or learning about Tesla's work with regard to Alternating Current and electromagnetic currents.

Perhaps the greatest ambition of Tesla was his dream to wirelessly transmit energy across long distances. He demonstrated that it was possible to wirelessly light up lamps using a method called inductive coupling, but he wasn't successful in building a long-range system to broadcast energy. If Tesla had his way, electricity would be free for everyone, but because his financial backers didn't like the idea of Tesla giving away his technology for free, JP Morgan (his primary source of funding) cut off his supply of money that would have eventually allowed Tesla's dream to perhaps come true.

In 1900, Tesla knew that we would one day be able to transmit information from one side of the Earth to the other, using a handheld wireless device. The system by which your mobile phone transmits information today was actually discovered by Tesla at the beginning of the twentieth century. Tesla was nominated for the Nobel Prize in physics for discovering the high frequency current and presenting electromagnetic rotating fields to us. Much of these electromagnetic waves were remnants of the big bang.

Tesla said that if you want to find the secrets of the universe, you must think in terms of energy, frequency, and vibration.

Tesla also went on to tell us that he was able to receive messages in the form of pictures in his mind when he was able to tap his subconscious into what we now call the universal consciousness. Essentially, Tesla was a psychic inventor whose inventions came to him through his psychic ability. The more he revealed his secret to the world, the more folks began to diminish and disregard his work as being crazy.

So, what does this have to do with meditation? Hang in there with me. I will get to it. I promise you. We first have to learn about another great man in history, Heinrich Rudolf Hertz.

Hertz was the first scientist to conclusively prove the existence of electromagnetic waves. The unit of frequency, or cycle per second, was eventually named the "Hertz" in his honor. For example, if something is said to be at a frequency of 60 Hz, then that wave can travel from point A to point B, and then back from point B to point A, exactly sixty times in a second.

Frequency is an important parameter used in science and engineering to specify the rate of oscillatory and vibratory phenomena.

The resonant frequency of the human brain typically varies between.05 Hz and 30 Hz. The lower end, or the.05, is perhaps a human brain in an extremely relaxed state of being. The higher the frequency of the brain, the more alert we are. With our ears, we can hear between 20 and 20,000 Hz. The human heart beats between 1 and 1.67 Hz. Everything in our reality has its own frequency, including the Earth.

The normal frequency of the Earth is usually 7.83 Hz. This may change slightly, however, by activity in the universe, such as a solar eclipse, a meteor shower, or a full moon. How many times have you felt "off" due to a full moon? If we are used to the Earth being at a constant frequency and then all of a sudden there is a small but distinctive change in frequency, it will disrupt our standing state of being.

So, back to meditation for a moment. This is my personal theory of how to achieve a beginning state of enlightenment, peace, and harmony between you and the universe.

What do you suppose would happen if you could go into a meditative state and alter or match your frequency precisely with that of Mother Earth? Both you and her at exactly 7.83 Hz, perfectly harmonious. This is where I think the magic happens. We are said to be in a telepathic state when the brain and Earth's frequencies are perfectly aligned. You'll know when you are there, you'll feel it inside you. Everything will have a way of coming together. It's when I have received many "aha" moments and gotten answers from the universe to my questions. It is truly one of many enlightened states of consciousness.

Frequencies play a key role in our relationships with others as well. Have you ever met someone and immediately felt like you bonded with this person after barely speaking to each other? You just knew this person was one you'd like to have in your life. Each of us operates on a default frequency, but we can change ours if we choose. Interactions with others' energy can change our frequency as well. Tesla went as far as to never shake another person's hand for fear of altering his energy. He was never married because he didn't want to be obligated to interact with another person regularly, especially one who could alter his frequency due to his emotional attachment.

Frequencies determine how we interact with energy beings that are deceased or in another realm as well. Matching frequencies make the transfer of information not only possible but also much easier. Information is a form of energy (we will discuss this in depth later in the book), and it can flow telepathically between all energy beings with ease when your frequencies or energies are aligned.

I'll say this again. Learn to meditate. It will change your life.

CHAPTER 15:

Aversion of Death

Let's return to the story of my speaking with Jessica's deceased dad, John, and the extremely important message he wanted to convey. His message wasn't easy to decipher at first. It wasn't until a few more messages came through that I could piece them together and work out that Jessica's dad was telling me he was worried about someone in his family and a serious health issue they had not been dealing with for a long time. If it wasn't dealt with sooner rather than later, the person would die. He wanted me to intervene and help.

So, one of my first premonitions was a life or death matter involving my girlfriend Jessica's family member! However, please bear in mind that at this point I had never met any of Jessica's family, as she was still in the final stages of her divorce and did not feel it was appropriate yet, which I respected and agreed with. Also, I had never been to medical school, and I knew nothing about medicine, medical treatments, or anything like that. How was I going to meet my girlfriend's family for the first time and tell one of them that they had a serious health issue that must be addressed quickly or something terrible could happen —and furthermore, I know this because I have been speaking to John, yes, the dead one. Do you think I'd ever be invited over for Thanksgiving dinner?

Who in their right mind was going to believe me? I didn't even believe me!

"Please!" (Journal Entry—Summer, 2019)

I felt Jessica's dad's presence in the room. I allowed my mind to drift off into an altered state, and I began to explain to him that I simply could not do what he was asking of me and to please remove the low vibrations that were inside and all around me. They were tortuous. I asked him to leave me be and to understand that I didn't know how I could help in this situation but that I understood his frustration. I pleaded with him to understand and go away.

Jessica's dad was with me almost every day at this time. I asked him, "If somehow, someway, I do this shit for you, what do I get out of it? What's in it for me?"

He broke out the movie screen with a large picture of Jessica smiling and said, "My daughter, you asshole! You get my daughter."

It was a Monday morning and, once again, there was John with something to tell me. I said, "John, please, I'm trying to run a fucking business here. I have to work! Can we talk later tonight?"

He listened to me and went away; I was surprised. So, like I promised, later that night when I was making myself a sandwich in my kitchen, I said, "Okay, John, tell me what's up." He did, and I ate my sandwich and went to bed. I was beginning to get the hang of this now.

"Pat on the Back" (Journal Entry—Summer, 2019)

Just days after this last talk with Jessica's dad, Jessica confided in me at dinner about her family member's health issue in great length and detail, asking me for guidance. I told her that I would help in any way I could.

The next night, Jessica and I spoke and, remarkably enough, there had been a circumstance that very day that had prompted more attention to the situation. We started to make a plan and I told her again what I had told her the day before, I would do whatever it takes to help.

Let me say that again because it is very significant. I said, "I'll do whatever it takes to help."

This set off a series of events in the next two hours, which included me feeling extremely high vibrations running through my body that I had never felt before, with euphoric qualities similar to those I experienced the day I died, was resuscitated, and returned to my body.

A vision of Jessica's dad came through with a big smile on his face and deep (Santa-like) laugh, saying, "I told you that you got this."

The feeling that was running through my body was almost indescribable. It was a warm, tingly high vibration sensation that tickled my body and brain. I began to laugh out loud, completely alone in my home office. I tried to control the laughter and rein it in a bit, but that proved to be nearly impossible. I acknowledged that it was certainly from John, and I was about to thank him and ask him to stop, but then I thought, Fuck that. This feels awesome.

Simply put, this was greater than anything I had ever felt (while alive). I truly hope all of you reading this will one day get to feel this feeling running through your entire being. It is incredible, and to think this was a reward for a job well done made it all the more valuable.

I sat in my high-back chair and simply enjoyed the feeling, which went on for almost twenty full minutes before I made it stop. I had to get back to the work I had been doing in the first place, so I thanked John for the gift and got back to my work.

I recalled that earlier that week Jessica had mentioned to me that she had been trying to get together with Medium Bonnie to have a reading done. They were going back and forth playing phone tag and trying to nail down a date and time that they could both do. The very same evening that I was feeling this amazing euphoria, Jessica received a text message from her medium, who set an appointment for the two of them to meet on June 18th at 11 AM. Furthermore, Jessica received this message at 11:11 PM. I have the actual screen shot to prove it! Here is the significance of this: June 18 is her dad's birthday and, as you know, 11:11 has been a constant communicative number between Jessica and her dad since he died.

My interpretation of this incident is that Jessica's father was extremely elated that he was making progress through me and gave me a "pat on the back," so to speak. The euphoric high vibrations were given to me as my reward, and he showed me a vision reassuring me that I *could* do this and that he was going to intervene as needed. He was letting me know that I was not expected to do this alone.

"Triple A" (Journal Entry—Winter, Late 2019)

It was November 2, 2019. I was driving to Jessica's mom's house to meet Jessica and her sister for dinner. Jessica was already there, so I was driving alone. It was about a two-hour drive with traffic. As I drove, I kept seeing John in my mind's eye. He would just kind of appear and then go away. He was smiling from ear to ear, happy with my accomplishments and that I was meeting some of Jessica's family. Halfway to my destination, I got a strong premonition that I had a flat tire. I saw words on the movie screen in my mind that read "flat tire." I didn't feel anything wrong with the car, so I began to think to myself, Please not that, not now. I checked my tire pressure from my dashboard while driving, and it was fine. I arrived at the house, parked my car, checked the tires, and they were still fine. We actually continued to use my car that evening to go to dinner and back. No problems. I could be wrong, couldn't I?

We came back to the house, and I parked my car outside and didn't move it until the next day. The following morning, I got in the car and we drove to get breakfast together and then returned to the house. Everything was still fine. We drove separately to her mom's house, so we also drove separately back home. I was alone in my car once again. I hate driving alone because I get hit with so many people's thoughts and various premonitions while I am driving. Sometimes I can get information about a person in one or more of the other cars around me and then I try to look at them.

An example of what I usually get is that the driver is talking on the phone while driving, or they are arguing with the person in the passenger seat. I also usually know when a car is going to cut me off and/or do something reckless. For this reason, it is very hard for me to drive long distances. Imagine getting hit with thoughts about people each time a car passes you or you pass by a car. Quite often, it will cause me to lose focus and drive past my exit or just drive a long distance out of my way because I get lost in these thoughts.

I sometimes have trouble turning them off when I am a captive audience for them. So many times, I have gotten completely lost by getting more involved mentally in what is happening in someone else's car than in my own.

Anyway, as I was driving home, I remembered the thought about the tire. It was more than a thought, and I knew that, but I didn't want it to be. I didn't check the tire pressure yet because I couldn't do anything about it, and I was hours from home. I didn't want to know if I was right at that moment in time, as it would just aggravate me the entire ride. I made it home, parked the car in front of my house and figured if it was flat, I would know in a few more hours.

I jumped into the car again the next morning and saw that the tire pressure was dropping. It was down more than ten pounds. I took it to the gas station, and they told me I had a slow leak due to a nail that had punctured the tire and was still in the tire. The fact that it hadn't come out of the tire is how I made it home all that distance. Couldn't I have been wrong just this once? Tires are very expensive.

My interpretation is that, more often than ever, I can get premonitions in real time, as things actually occur. I am not sure if Jessica's dad was specifically present to send me this message of the flat tire, or if he was just present for the first time I was to meet his family. Either way, I had asked the universe to let me get home, and it came through for me.

"I Did It, John" (Journal Entry—Winter, Late 2019)

It was November 7, 2019. Jessica's family member had agreed to address the health issue that John was insisting I help with. It was now Thursday night, and the initial appointment was scheduled for the following Tuesday. Jessica and I were both uneasy about this person being alone before her appointment, as everyone was feeling nervous. I told Jessica I would meditate to see if I could get anything that would indicate if she was okay.

I lay down on my bed and within minutes I felt a connection to another realm. It had been getting really easy to connect lately if I wanted to receive messages. The more I did it, the easier it got, which was what Medium Bonnie had told me would happen. Exercising the ability makes it much easier. I immediately heard what has been called light language by other mediums, which is similar to a ringing in the ears. It often fluctuates in pitch and in volume. For some reason, I get the sound as soon as I connect these days, and it occurs almost every time I meditate. I will discuss light language in more detail later in the book, but for now, you only need to know that it is a form of communication from the other side.

I remained connected with the sound and asked my guides to tell me what I needed to know.

I was now no longer in my bed but in this person's home. With my mind's eye, I began looking around. The sound of light language was changing in pitch and volume. It would go higher and lower as I moved around the house in my mind.

I asked my question repeatedly. I continued to look and then I saw a vision. This person was feeling agitated, anxious, and depressed, and these feelings had magnified intensely over the days she would potentially be alone. As I saw this in my mind's eye, the sound of the light language increased to being really loud and unbearable. I understood that this individual needed her people to be around her during this time, although would not come out and ask for this, but rather insist being fine.

I thanked my guides, opened my eyes, and returned to my bed. I looked over at the television, and it was a news broadcast about people who were dying in larger numbers in America from the same thing this person was dealing with, when left untreated. That was simply much too coincidental to be anything other than a secondary direct message confirming what I had just been told.

I called Jessica and she took the necessary steps to handle the situation. She did this without telling anyone what I saw. At this point, I was not ready to tell anyone what I could do.

What was missing from this vision, however, was the extremely low vibrations that usually accompany an ominous or negative premonition. Why was that missing this time? The light language became excruciatingly loud and uncomfortable, but that was different from the way I usually get alerted to really bad shit.

My interpretation is that this message came from my guides and/or masters and not Jessica's dad. I think that is why the vibrations weren't present during the vision. I must continue learning to interpret the light language as to what pitch or volume can be associated with good, bad, or indifferent messages.

You'll be happy to know that all went very well...... Maybe I will be invited to Thanksgiving dinner after all.

CHAPTER 16:

Doolittle I'm Not

I have a complicated relationship with animals. I like them as long as they aren't mine. I don't want to care for them, I suppose, and I especially do not like needy animals that require lots of love and attention. It's just too much work, and I don't like clingy things that can't support themselves. I don't dislike them, but I can do without them.

I am fond of cats, however. They take care of themselves, and they don't really need humans all that much. They also have the ability to see energies that enter the room. I had a cat as a pet once. I was completely distraught the day I had to put her to sleep. She was old and had terminal cancer. I have been to at least fourteen or fifteen human funerals and kept my shit together, but when that cat died, I broke down. I was devastated.

Many animals have a somewhat developed sixth sense. They lack the conscious mind that humans have to analyze and make sense of things, but they have some insight into the metaphysical world. If you want to know if you are being visited by an energy being that you cannot see, get a cat. They will always let you know.

A cat can go from sleeping soundly to jumping up and staring at the blank wall intently without blinking. It isn't because something fascinating on the wall woke them out of a sound sleep. It is because you have a visitor that the cat can see or sense.

Cats can also tell you a great deal about your friends. See your cat's reaction to the different people who enter your home. Then keep track of the ones that your cat liked versus the ones your cat didn't like. You will learn which ones are good friends and which have an evil side to them or which will betray you at some point in life. I venture to bet that if you keep track, your cat will be over ninety-five percent accurate on this.

Due to the business I am in, I enter many people's homes on a regular basis. Many of the homes have pets. Quite often, I will hear things like, "Please don't try to pet my dog. She will bite."

"Okay," I say, "I won't." However, within five minutes of sitting on their couch, this so-called mean animal will come and sit on my lap and lick me.

I have had many pet owners tell me, "I cannot believe my dog won't bark at you. My dog hates other people."

"I know," I say. "I get that a lot."

The same goes for cats or any animal, for that matter.

"Hi, nice to meet you," I say.

"Come right in," they say, "but please don't try to pet the cat. She scratches and bites everyone." Five minutes into our conversation, the cat is on my lap purring and about to fall asleep on top of me. Every place I go. Every single time. Each and every animal will come up to me and relax within about five minutes of me being there. They feel safe with me for some reason. Maybe they know I can see things that they can see and feel, things that perhaps make them uneasy, and they feel protected. I'm really not sure. I have no desire to take care of an animal again, and yet everywhere I go they attach themselves to me. This isn't just about dogs and cats. This is all animals.

I was in Las Vegas at the hotel that had a dolphin show many years ago. We went back to meet the dolphins. There were about eight of us on this special tour. I walked away from the pool to take a call on my mobile phone. Everyone was far away from me playing with the dolphins and giving them attention when I suddenly got hit on the back of the head with a basketball. I turned around, and the dolphin started laughing at me. My friend was looking at me.

I said, "Why did you hit me with the ball, you jerk?"

He said, "I didn't do it. The dolphin did."

I said, "Get the fuck out of here and stop messing around. I am on the phone."

I threw the ball far into the water so my friend couldn't hit me again with it, and I turned around again to continue my phone call. Bam! Again, I was hit in the back of the head with the ball, and now there were two dolphins laughing at me. My friend was laughing hysterically as well.

I said, "What the hell, man? I threw the ball to the other side of the pool. How did you get it?"

He said, "I didn't. It was the dolphins! That's what I was trying to tell you."

I hung up the call. There were two dolphins looking at me with their heads above the water. I told my friend to walk away, then I picked up the ball and threw it into the pool again. One dolphin went and got the ball and threw it back to me. *Kikikiky.* That is a dolphin laugh. It sounds hysterical. I threw it back and they returned it to me.

This went on a few more times. I gave the ball to my friend and told him to throw it to the dolphins. The dolphin got the ball back but threw it to me, not my friend.

My friend said, "They love you for some reason."

Even the dolphin trainer came over to see if I was giving them food or something. They followed me as far as they could as I walked along the pool to the exit. *Kikikiky.* All the other tourists were on the other side, and the dolphins came to see me.

This type of craziness with animals has always been there. When I went to Arkansas for the psychic retreat, the woman who owns and runs the dome in the Hot Springs area told me that all animals can recognize psychic abilities in humans, and they attach themselves immediately to people who have it. The animal feels protected more so by the human. I had one of those "Aha" moments right then and there.

The first time I was at Jessica's house, she had two cats, one dog, a ferret, and a fish tank. I was on the couch as Jessica left me for a moment and went to the bathroom. When she returned, the one cat was on my shoulder licking my ear, the other cat (who hates people, mind you) was on my lap asleep, the dog was lying down at my feet looking up at me, and the ferret had gotten loose.

CHAPTER 17:

Clear Cut

A spiritual clearing is done because everyone encounters negativity in life, including pain, turmoil, troubles at work, break-ups, and other losses. These negative events can block the flow of energy in your body if you allow them to build and gather power. By performing a spiritual clearing or cleansing, you can release these negatives and reclaim your power and energy flow.

As you know, my spiritual clearing was done by Nicole. If you are having this done, you need not be present at the time, but they will tell you the day and the approximate time of day it will be performed. They do this because you will feel it happening. She told me in advance not to make any appointments the day of the clearing and not to make any life-altering decisions for a few days until it all settled. Mine felt very uplifting. I could tell it was being done, and for a few days thereafter I was a little bit "off" mentally, but that means it was working. Within two days, I was back to myself and actually felt revitalized.

Since I had a good experience with this, I decided to take it to the next level and go in and see Nicole in her office. In this session, I lay down on a table. There was incense and sage burning in the room. She asked the assistance of the archangels to be present during the process. She touched each chakra with her hand, and as she did so, it opened a clear path to allow the flow of energy through each. When I was there, I didn't even know what a chakra was. In case you don't either, here is what they are and what they do.

Chakras are the energy centers of the body. They are the circular vortexes of energy that are placed in seven different points on the spinal column. They start at the perineum (the space between the genitals and anus) and run up in a straight line to the top of the head. The topmost chakra is in fact on the top of the head (the crown) and continues just outside of the body above the top of the head. These chakras are responsible for regulating life energy, which is also known as prana.

The function of the chakras is to spin and draw in this energy to keep the spiritual, mental, emotional, and physical health of the body in balance.

I admittedly knew nothing about chakras until I had an attunement, so I had to do research to educate myself about what a chakra was. Just because I have certain abilities, I am not yet an expert on all things metaphysical. Here are the seven chakras as I learned them:

-The Root Chakra: The foundation of your body, the root chakra is sturdy, stabilizing, and supportive, keeping everything safely connected as long as it's functioning properly. It's associated with the base of the spine, the pelvic floor, and the first three vertebrae, and it's responsible for an individual's sense of security and survival. Because of that, it's also connected to whatever you use to ground yourself, including basic needs, such as food, water, shelter, and safety, as well as your more emotional needs, such as letting go of fear and feeling safe. As you well know, when these needs are met, you tend to worry less. When it's blocked, a variety of ailments can occur, including anxiety disorders and fears.

-The Sacral Chakra: Located above the pubic bone and below the navel, this chakra is responsible for our sexual and creative energies, and it's associated with the color orange and the element of water. When your sacral chakra is aligned, you will likely feel great. You'll be friendly, passionate, and successfully fulfilled, and you'll elicit feelings of wellness, abundance, pleasure, and joy. When it's blocked, however, you'll feel uninspired creatively or have some emotional instability. This chakra can also be associated with physical sexual dysfunction, and you could experience a fear of change, depression, or addiction-like behaviors.

-The Solar Plexus Chakra: The third chakra is said to be your source of individual power, ruling over self-esteem. It is the action and balance chakra that focuses on individual willpower, personal power, and commitment. It is located from the navel to about the ribcage. When it is blocked, you can suffer from low self-esteem, have difficulty making decisions, and may have anger or control issues.

-The Heart Chakra: As the central chakra, the fourth chakra, found at the center of your chest, represents where the physical and the spiritual meet. It is all about love. Associated with the colors green and pink, it's believed that when your heart chakra is aligned and balanced, love and compassion are flowing freely—both in terms of giving it out and getting it back. When it's blocked, a closed heart chakra can give way to grief, anger, jealousy, fear of betrayal, and hatred toward yourself and others—especially in the form of holding a grudge against something or someone.

-The Throat Chakra: Your fifth chakra is all about speaking your inner truth—or, more specifically, ensuring that your inner truths are properly communicated. The throat chakra rules all communication. When this chakra is in check, you're able to fully listen, speak, and express yourself clearly. When it's blocked, in addition to having trouble speaking your truth, you will find it hard to pay attention and stay focused, and you might fear judgment from others.

-The Third-Eye Chakra: The third-eye chakra is your sixth chakra and is physically located between your eyebrows. It governs your intuition plus the ability to recognize and tap into it. The third eye is also said to be responsible for all things between you and the outside world, serving as a bridge between the two, and allowing you to cut through illusions and drama to see the clear picture. When it's blocked, you may have trouble accessing your intuition, trusting your inner voice, recalling important facts, or learning new skills. And if your lower chakras—i.e., the root, sacral, solar plexus, and heart chakras—are unbalanced, your third eye will likely be as well, which may cause you to be more judgmental, dismissive, and introverted. A third-eye blockage is associated with a broad range of issues, including depression, anxiety, and a more judgmental attitude.

-The Crown Chakra: This is the center of enlightenment and our direct connection to our higher selves, others, and ultimately, the divine. As the name suggests, the seventh chakra is located at the crown of your head. When aligned, the realizations that occur within you are said to be along the lines of pure awareness, consciousness, and all-expansive, bigger than yourself and yet part of one giant universe. A crown chakra blockage may create feelings of isolation or emotional distress and a feeling of being disconnected from everyone and everything. You might feel like your normal self, just not in a state of connection and enlightenment. Unlike the other chakras, the crown chakra is often opened up fully through specific meditative exercises, which takes practice. You may be able to work on it through daily meditation, moments of silence, and gratitude, to have those moments of spiritual connection.

Let's return to my energy healing, which was my visit to Nicole's office in New Jersey. When Nicole first touched the top of my head, I immediately felt a very hot sensation travel through it like a lightning bolt. It just kept getting hotter and hotter. Next, she touched my forehead or my "third eye." This made my entire head feel like it was on fire and my insides tremble. She moved to my throat and then heart chakras. I felt a little more at ease then, but my head was still hot.

Then she touched the solar plexus chakra. This is when I began to shake uncontrollably on the table. I could not stop it from happening. I tried, but it just got worse. Remember that this chakra is where anger and control issues come into play.

I continued to shake violently, almost bouncing up and down on the table. You would have thought it had now become an exorcism. Was green shit going to spew from my mouth next? She moved down to the remaining chakras, and it was then that all the shaking stopped. I left there feeling very lightheaded but also very relieved. Something very positive had transformed inside of me, but it would be a little while for me to see the actual results that were coming.

I felt like something had opened up. There was a new flow of energy that hadn't been there before in the crown of my head. This would become very significant, as it is where much of my information comes through. It is also what would later trigger another out-of-body experience. During this one, however, I was very much alive.

CHAPTER 18:

Head Like a Hole

I had been working on one of Medium Bonnie's suggestions for a meditating exercise whereby I picture a thermometer in my mind and as the temperature rises, I bring myself into more of a metaphysical state while leaving my body, so to speak. I had been trying this daily since she and I had met weeks before, but with limited success. I would get from zero to twenty degrees and then maybe to forty degrees at best, but then go right back down to twenty very quickly. I couldn't maintain it. I felt the separation from the physical to the metaphysical as I went higher up on the thermometer, but it was quite difficult for me to get there and remain there.

"Shut It Down" (Journal Entry—Summer, 2019)

It was the night of August 15, 2019. I was very tired but couldn't sleep, so I was watching television at about 10 PM. I was watching a television series that I liked and followed, so I was very interested in it. Out of nowhere, I began to have a very high vibration in my head and above my head. The part about "above my head" is important here. Up until now, most vibrations had been low, located between my waist and my knees, and the highest ones I could recall went up to my head from my chest. The higher the vibration and the higher the part of my body affected, the better or more positive the message seemed to be. This was my assessment at the time.

Therefore, at first, I thought this message must be really good, as it felt almost euphoric. It came on very quickly, however, much quicker than ever before. The speed was alarming to me, so I tried to slow it down at first. When that didn't work, I tried to stop it completely and go back to watching my television show. Someone or something had other plans for me this night, however.

I tried to refocus on the television, but I began to see lines shooting across the room. This has happened to me often. I see a shooting dark line or a white swirly line in my peripheral vision only, and then the feeling of the room changes, as if I am not alone. When I used to have a cat, the cat and I would be the only two in the room who could see the line as it shot across the room faster than you could blink before it was gone. If the cat didn't hiss or mind the line, then I didn't care either.

On this particular night, I could see many lines moving about the room every few minutes. This was alarming to me because, while I often come home to one or two lines, I had never seen this many. They seemed to be everywhere. For just a fraction of a second, I'd see these dark lines or white swirly lines shoot across in one side of my vision and then disappear. My room felt like it was filled with lines; they were everywhere. I felt like I was alone in a crowded room. I was completely frozen with fear and couldn't move from my position on the bed.

I closed my eyes as I sat curled up in one corner of my bed. I couldn't move my body. I began to go higher and higher on the thermometer. If you recall, the thermometer was an exercise that Medium Bonnie gave me to work on. This time, however, I wasn't "doing" this per se; it was just happening to me. I was going higher on the thermometer without consciously doing the work myself. In hindsight, it was the most amazing positive, semi-euphoric feeling I had experienced in a long while, but it was super scary as shit at the same time! A part of me went up into the high vibrations that were above my head and left my body. My "energy," or my consciousness, had left my physical body!

This was the first time I saw my second-to-top-level spirit guides. Once I closed my eyes on that bed, I floated up to them easily. It was like they were pulling my consciousness toward them until I was standing directly in front of them. They appeared to me as silver, black, and white lines inside of a gold perimeter that held the lines together. They had no bodies or faces, just brightly lit gold shells filled with these silver, black, and white lines. There was an entire panel of them, so to speak. Seven beings in a straight line. I could tell that the one in the center was the leader of the panel, and I could feel their power. Collectively, it was immense. Some of them were confused as to why I wanted this to stop since I had been practicing using Medium Bonnie's techniques and asking for this to evolve daily, but this experience was so overpowering and frightening that I just wanted it to end. I had never expected or even remotely experienced anything of this magnitude before. This was so powerful, and it had happened so quickly without warning. All the preparation in the world wouldn't have prepared me for what was to come next. I remembered Medium Bonnie always telling me, however, that I was in control. She would tell me this repeatedly. So, I said over and over, "If I am in control, shut it down now! If I am in control, shut it down now!" I got more forceful each time I said it.

It didn't shut down, however, so I wasn't sure I actually had control like Medium Bonnie had said.

My consciousness was no longer in my bed. My body was still there, of course, but my mind wasn't. I was allowed to return to check on my body during this time. I know I did that at least twice, and it gave me some confidence and peace knowing I was able to do so. It gave me the courage to continue.

My mind was now overlooking a boardwalk on a beautiful sunny morning. No one was out yet. There were no people present. I wondered why they had placed me here and what they wanted me to see. I was scared, but I had calmed a bit, so I decided to see how much control I actually had here. Mind you, this was unlike any other experience I had ever had, except for when I died and came back to life. I felt like I could move around out of my body. I was high up and looking down. I could control how high up I went. I was floating energy (just like the lines I had seen in my bedroom before I got here), and I could move at what I thought was the speed of light, again, just like the lines in my bedroom. Had I become a line in someone else's realm of existence?

I decided to move to another section of the boardwalk that was far off in the distance, and I moved in what seemed to be a split second. Somehow,

I knew I had gone exactly one mile down the boardwalk and stopped. I didn't want to go any further. I was testing to see if I had control. I did the same again, up the boardwalk one mile, and returned to my original position. After doing this one more time, going up and proceeding to come back, I saw something at five eighths of a mile back on the return. It appeared to be a ramp or a bridge on that exact spot of the boardwalk. It went from the eastern edge of the boardwalk, up into the sky, and over the ocean. I couldn't see what was on the other end from my vantage point. The only way for me to know what was there was to go over it. It seemed less of an actual structure that we are used to and more of a direction for me to follow because the entire ramp was made of something I could see through. It would take me higher into the clouds and over the water. I began to go up the ramp, and as I did, I felt increasingly powerful, but at the same time, I was completely petrified. Where did they want me to go? Who wanted me to experience this? Would I ever be able to come back?

The ramp, as it turned out, would have taken me over the ocean. I fear the water, particularly the ocean. I nearly drowned in the ocean as a kid, and I never went back in the ocean after that. So, I stopped myself just a little way up the ramp. I paused in panic and demanded to go back. If in fact I was in control, then I could come back here to this point whenever I wanted to on my terms. I went back to hovering over the boardwalk again, away from the ramp. Since I was able to bring myself back off the ramp, I felt a little more confident and in control. I waited there for a minute, and then proceeded to head back up the ramp just a little farther than the last time. I really wanted to see what was on the other side, but then I looked down at the water. Remember, I could see through the ramp. I became too frightened once again, and I came back to land. This time, however, I came all the way back. Back down into my bed, into my room, and back to my television show.

Still frozen in fear, I remember I had to use the bathroom, but I did not dare move out of my bed. I then demanded everything and anything around me to go away and leave me be. There are two emotions that I do not deal with very well. Sadness and fear. I immediately turn them into anger because I know how to be angry. The lines didn't listen the first time. Again, I said it, with conviction and force "get the fuck out of here!" And then it was done. The lines went away, or at least most of them did. One or two hung around, but that was normal. The panic ended, and I tried to take my mind off it and finish watching my show. There was no way I could sleep now though. I would process what happened to me tomorrow. For the time being, I needed to just rest and recover.

By the way, one of the most bizarre things I noticed was that the show I had been watching before the experience started had not advanced by more than about a minute. It was almost like I'd paused it. Thirty to forty seconds in our time seemed like thirty to forty minutes in that realm.

I eventually fell asleep, and I woke up having more confidence in myself and my ability to control this.

My interpretation is that this was meant to be a positive experience for me, but because I did not initiate it or feel like I had control, I panicked. Why did it happen this way? Why did it happen on that day? What was the message? I still have many unanswered questions about this experience.

CHAPTER 19:

Ladies and Gentlemen, Meet the Clairs!

Before writing this book, I had no knowledge of this stuff, so I had to do much of my own research and, with the help of Medium Bonnie, learn to navigate this newfound territory. The "Clairs" are the different senses in the metaphysical world.

Ask any psychic what is their least favorite word and they will probably tell you "psychic." The term has become synonymous with fraud. I hate referring to myself that way. The term has given a really bad name to the study of parapsychology. The frauds also make it more difficult for us to get any real funding for research on the subject of parapsychology—research I so desperately need.

Please remember that I was the biggest skeptic to ever walk this Earth. If these events hadn't happened to me, I would without doubt still be a nonbeliever. I can only do so much research on my own. We need to get real scientific studies completed to validate and learn everything about this phenomenon once and for all.

If you meet me, you'll see that I do not look like a typical spiritual person. I just look like a regular guy who dresses up and goes to work each day. I love my work, I love my kids, and I love my life. Nothing about me suggests I have any abilities whatsoever. I'm just your average everyday businessman on the surface.

I have an overwhelming feeling, however, that I must use this ability to help others, and I try my best to do so. I think that is why it is growing exponentially and quite rapidly. Believe me when I tell you I am no martyr, but for some reason I feel that if I continue to focus on helping others, I will receive something I need in return. I believe I have these abilities because I use them for good.

My guides (whoever they may be) have helped me stay alive many times and kept me away from danger. For that, I'm eternally grateful, but I have never sat down and begun to meditate on whether I am going to get that promotion, or that raise, or anything superficial like that.

I think there may be many other people out there similar to me and that is why I write this. Meaning we all have a sixth sense. We were born with it. Some are just more capable of using it than others. If you, like me, have gotten hit with unexplainable events, visions, or premonitions, you are probably not crazy. You are different, but you are normal at the same time. Your conscious mind is simply more evolved. Someday, all humans will be able to interact with other realms and other levels of consciousness. It isn't that far off in the future, in my opinion. I'm not prepared to put a time frame on it just yet, but I believe the time will come. Each generation will become more advanced than the last.

You have this. Everyone does. You just need to "tap" into it and further develop it. One day, I may help you with this, but I must first master it myself. By no means have I mastered this yet.

So, let's get back to the focus of this chapter and allow me to introduce to you the Clairs.

The Clair Senses

These words refer to psychic sensitivity abilities corresponding to the various human senses, such as seeing, hearing, feeling, smelling, tasting, and touching. The Clair senses in psychic terms are as follows: clairvoyance, clairaudience, clairsentience, clairscent, clairtangency, clairgustance, clairempathy, and channeling. The following are brief explanations of each one.

Clairvoyance (clear vision)—The ability to reach into another vibrational frequency and visually perceive "within the mind's eye" something existing in that realm. A clairvoyant is one who receives extrasensory impressions and symbols in the form of "inner sight" or mental images, which are perceived without the aid of the physical eyes and beyond the limitations of ordinary time and space. These impressions are more easily perceived in an alpha state and during meditation, though many clairvoyants can obtain visual information regarding the past, present, and future in a variety of environments.

Clairaudience (clear audio/hearing)—The ability to perceive sounds or words and extrasensory noise from sources broadcast from another realm in the form of "inner ear" or mental tones, which are perceived without the aid of the physical ear and beyond the limitations of ordinary time and space. These tones and vibrations are more easily perceived in an alpha state and during meditation, though many clairaudients can obtain verbal and sound-related information regarding the past, present, and future in a variety of environments. Most mediums work with both clairvoyance and clairaudience.

Clairsentience (clear sensation or feeling)—The ability to perceive information by a "feeling" of emotion within the whole body, without any outer stimuli related to the feeling or information (see also clairempathy).

Clairscent (clear smelling)—The ability to smell a fragrance/odor of substance or food that is not in one's surroundings. These odors are perceived without the aid of the physical nose and beyond the limitations of ordinary time and space.

Clairtangency (clear touching)—Also known as psychometry, this is the ability to handle an object or touch an area and perceive through the palms of one's hands information about the article or its owner that was not previously known by the clairtangent.

Clairgustance (clear tasting)—The ability to taste a substance without putting anything in one's mouth. It is claimed that those who possess this ability are able to perceive the essence of a substance from the other realms through taste.

Clairempathy (clear emotion)—An empath is a person who can psychically tune into the emotional experience of a person, place, or animal. Clairempathy is a type of telepathy that enables someone to sense or feel within one's self the attitude, emotion, or ailment of another person or entity. Empaths tune into the vibrations and "feel" the tones of the aura.

Channel/Channeling

Channel—A person who allows their body and mind to be used as a mechanism for other world intelligence and bring information or healing energy to others.

Channeling—The ability to allow an energy-based intelligence to enter one's mind and impress thoughts upon the consciousness to be spoken aloud, using one's voice or body to deliver the information or energy.

To date, I have experienced many of these, but by the time you read this book, who the hell knows what else I might have experienced? Things have been opening up in very rapid succession. I am already doing things now that I couldn't do when I first started writing this book. Every time I have a learning session with Medium Bonnie, something new seems to open up. It's almost as if she is controlling how much water comes at me out of a spigot each time, so I won't drown.

There is a distinct difference in receiving a premonition when in an altered state of mind, such as a "daydream" type, versus going into a deeper meditation and speaking with the deceased or guides. These visions can be in the past, present, or future, as you will see. Below are premonitions that I received while in an altered state of trance.

"Stop Him" (Journal Entry—Winter, Late 2018)

Jessica and I were driving down the street and we passed by one of her family's retail stores. Her dad and his business partner had owned it for many years, but after his death, they needed a manager to run things.

"Who runs it for your mom?" I said.

Jessica replied, "Jerry. He has been there for many years and is close with our family."

We were lying in bed about a week or so later, and she mentioned the hardware store again. I saw this as an opportunity to tell her what I saw in my mind's eye when we drove past the store.

I saw a man with his back to me in a checkered shirt, maybe flannel, with cash in hand and ringing up 0.00 on a cash register.

I said, "Can you trust Jerry the manager of the store?"

She said, "Yes, absolutely, without question."

"I don't think you should."

"Why?"

"I think you may need to take a second look at him; he may be stealing."

"No way," Jessica replied. "We have known Jerry for years, and he would never."

I never mentioned what I saw. I just let it be. After all, what if I was wrong?

Several weeks later, Jessica asked me if I knew of anyone who could possibly manage the store.

"Why?" I asked.

"Jerry was fired and arrested for stealing from the store," Jessica said.

My interpretation of the vision was that it was a symbol of theft. However, I did not tell Jessica I had a vision at that time. I just said it was a gut feeling because I really didn't think I fully understood what was happening to me back then. I told Jessica I get a lot of these gut feelings and that they are usually accurate.

"The Betrayal" (Journal Entry—Spring, 2019)

In another vision, I saw two people standing side by side looking down at their cell phones and laughing. One of them was someone we both knew and did not like very much, but the other I did not know until I met one of Jessica's friends many weeks after this vision came to me. While I was physically present and in the same room with this person, I received very low, deep vibrations, which typically means danger or stay away. I had trouble touching her or shaking her hand. It was so strong. I was then able to confirm that she had been the female in the vision, and I knew was very capable of betrayal.

I was really tormented about whether to tell Jessica about this. Would I be the cause of the ending the friendship? I never want to do that. In addition, what if I was wrong? However, I know that I should not doubt myself because each time I do, my information comes back to me as being accurate. I was torn and didn't know what to do.

Then, one day, a conversation came up about someone betraying Jessica's trust. It was a different person, but I saw an opening. I began to tell her about what I'd seen, and she was not at all surprised. I asked her why she wasn't taking this seriously. She said because that person I was referring to had already betrayed her. The woman had apologized for it many times over, and Jessica had accepted her apology. I was greatly relieved that I wasn't telling Jessica something she didn't already know.

"The Prediction" (Journal Entry—Summer, 2019)

Jessica was nervous about an upcoming court hearing. She expressed to me that she was uncertain about the outcome. She asked me to try and use my abilities to get her some information on what would transpire. Of course I cared about her, but I was not sure of my abilities at this point. You will continually see in this book a pattern of me doubting myself. Even to this day I ask myself, How can this be real? If it is real, why me?

Anyway, up until this point in time, I had never given a prediction that I had initiated. In other words, all the things I had seen prior to this were given to me at random. I hadn't asked for them. That being said, however, if there was any possibility that I could get some information that would put her mind at ease, I would do so.

So, I told her, "I am going to take a shot at this. I will relay what I get back to you, but please don't hold me to it."

She said, "Of course not."

"Okay, let me see if I can get anything for you."

I went into a meditative state and tried to get a visual. Surprisingly, I got something relatively quickly. I think it was quickly, anyway. Sometimes I lose track of time in a meditation. In the following journal entry, I explain what I saw and how I believe I received this particular information.

"Does This Thing Work?" (Journal Entry—Summer, 2019)

Jessica's court hearing was the next day. This was the first time ever that I was going to give someone an actual premeditated prediction and then wait to see if it came true. Then I would better understand how much of this was real and if I had any control over it. (I still disbelieved at this point that this was real.)

In my premonition, I saw Jessica walking out of the court with her arms in a "V" like victory. Furthermore, I saw her opponent with their head down and a look of defeat. I explained my interpretation to her, "You will win in the short term here. On this particular court date, most, if not all, will go your way. Your opponent will be more beaten down than angry as a result of this. The opposing lawyer will attack you and your character personally. It will be difficult to withstand, but you will win and afterward you'll feel better. By no means will you have won the war, but you will win this particular battle. Go in with thick skin and ignore the words and enjoy the fact that you will be victorious at the very least for this one day."

I could not wait to hear what happened in court from Jessica because I was rooting for her, of course, but also because I needed validation. Could I actually do this?

Jessica said that the judge had ruled fourteen out of the fourteen motions in her favor, but she sounded sad and I asked why. She went on to tell me of the horrific lies the opposing counsel said about her in the courtroom and how badly that had affected her.

I said, "Try to be happy about the win and not let the other shit get to you."

It turned out I was a hundred percent correct and it blew my mind.

My interpretation is that I was able to see what would happen in this case based upon what the other people involved were thinking or feeling. It was just easier for me to know what was happening in the other person's mind. Most people know if they will win or lose something before a contest. I am just tapping into what they already know or think. I saw the loss from the opponent's viewpoint and the personal attack coming at her.

"The Prediction Part 2—Follow Up" (Journal Entry—Winter, Late 2019)

Jessica had received three important checks, one per month for the past three months. I told her she would receive exactly three checks in a previous premonition. All three checks had now come, and I saw them previously being represented in my vision by a legal-sized envelope in my mind's eye delivered to her mailbox. Many things I see are metaphorical and must be deciphered to get the true meaning. She had indeed received the three checks but not necessarily in the mail and not necessarily in a legal-sized envelope. You'll understand what I am saying momentarily. As we approached the fourth month, Jessica asked me again to use my ability to "look and see" whether her monthly checks would continue or not. I agreed to look into it and began to meditate. I saw a letter-sized envelope being delivered to her in the fourth month the same way as the legal-sized ones had come to her. Keep in mind that a legal-sized envelope is larger than a letter-sized envelope, as this will prove to be an important factor.

Since it was a smaller size, it could represent a partial check or a letter saying something about the status of the fourth check and/or future checks. I explained to her that December 9 and December 11 were significant in relation to the checks, and she would have all her answers by then.

A few days before December 9th, Jessica got a last-minute message to meet her lawyer in a mediation meeting. She was told to be at the judge's office on December 9. By the end of that day, they had reached a settlement, and both parties had until December 11 to sign and submit the agreement to the judge. The settlement was the best possible outcome. Regarding the smaller envelope that was coming in the fourth month, it came on December 18, 2019, and it was a partial check; hence, the vision of the smaller-sized envelope.

My interpretation is that I can "see" what tomorrow will bring in some cases, and I may as well begin accepting this as my new reality.

CHAPTER 20:

A Spiritual Resort to Refresh and Revitalize

Jessica and I went to a resort in Monticello, NY. It was such an amazing place to go and meditate, do yoga, get massages, exercise, and swim all day in pools with waterfalls. There is no alcohol. No clubs. No night-life. Bedtime is 10 PM, and wake-up time is 6 AM. This is a true yogi/Buddhist-based resort. The first time we went, I was excited for the new experience. I never drink alcohol and prefer daytime to nighttime. I thought this must be the perfect place for me.

On the way there, Jessica told me the food was one hundred percent vegan. I can tell you she purposely waited until we drove halfway up a frigging mountain in Upstate NY to tell me this part.

"I'm so sorry, Jessica, but I think I misheard you. Did you say all the food was vegan?"

"Yes," she replied.

"Correct me if I am wrong, but that means no meat, right? So, no fucking sausage then!" I exclaimed. I am an Italian from New Jersey!

What the hell did I sign up for? I had not subscribed to the whole peace, love, and harmony thing yet. I thought peace was a little overrated, personally.

Long story short, we had a five-star chef prepare our vegan food the entire time we were there. I was allowed eggs for breakfast, so it was a good compromise, and I now love vegan food! It was absolutely delicious. I did not see that coming. I wish I could remember the chef's name to give them credit here. The host of the restaurant was spectacular as well. He could remember the name of every guest staying at the resort. Each time a guest walked in, he would immediately greet them with a smile and call them individually by their first names to welcome them. We felt like royalty each time we entered the dining room. He must have had one of those photographic memories. Brilliant!

"You Still Need Proof?" (Journal Entry—Fall, 2019)

Throughout our weekend there, Jessica and I had many conversations about what had been happening. We'd had enough experiences by this point to realize we had to take this seriously, but I still had doubts. On the last night, we were sitting on a loveseat in our room looking out at the view. It was dark outside, but we could see the mountains lit up in the distance. Jessica asked me, "How important is it for you to use this ability to help others?"

My reply was again something to the effect of, "What if this isn't real? What if this is all an illusion brought on by events made up by my subconscious? How do I know it is real? What if it's not real? Can this really be real? It's quite crazy."

And with that statement, all the electricity went out in the room. The TV went off, all the lights, and everything was out. We were in complete darkness. Jessica laughed and said, "Oh My God!" Looking out our window, however, we could see the other hotel guests still had their lights on. Our lights came back on after about 30 seconds, and Jessica was now almost standing up on the couch with her arms up in the air and smiling a huge smile at me.

"Do you still need more proof?"

"I guess not," I said.

Something similar happened a second time while there, and with that I apologized to the universe for doubting. I needed to believe. I now knew this. Everything was changing.

My interpretation is that every now and then I still revert back to doubting myself. My analytical mind wants to think this can't really be happening, but it is harder and harder to deny. Also, as I continue to compare my experiences with others, the similarities are uncanny. I went into this never studying or reading a book about it, and yet I am experiencing the exact same things in the exact same way as those who claim to have these gifts.

"You Still Need Proof?" Pt. 2 (Journal Entry—Fall, 2019)

The following day at the resort, Jessica and I decided to go for a small hike after breakfast. It was late summer, changing slowly into fall, so the temperature was mild and perfect. The sun was beading down upon us as we walked through the wooded trail in complete isolation. There wasn't a cloud in the sky, and there was almost no breeze. It was absolutely perfect. Everything was perfect. Life was great, and we were grateful for this moment together.

We walked the trail to a man-made fire pit with a bench overlooking it and the lake in front of us. With our arms around each other, we began talking about her dad making contact and its meaning and importance. I couldn't help but bring back my self-doubt. It crept up on me over and over again. Whenever our conversation went deep into me speaking with dead people or seeing premonitions of things, I just had to stop myself from speaking or I'd ask her the same question repeatedly: "What if this isn't real? What if it is all in my head? What if it isn't your dad?"

She said, "Well then, it would all be in my head too, and that is less likely since I am just an observer."

I began to say something that began with, "Yes, but…," but before I could complete my next sentence, the trees began to shake as the wind picked up on this picture-perfect day. It got stronger and stronger and began to kind of swirl around us with more and more force. We were no longer speaking, just witnessing this in dumbfounded silence. The wind picked up more speed, not a cloud in the frigging sky, and now all the trees above us were shaking. Neither of us could move. The trees above us were some fifty feet high and swaying back and forth as though a hurricane was coming through. There wasn't even a drop of rain in the forecast and still not one cloud in the sky. This continued for several minutes as we sat there, in awe, hugging each other. Jessica was smiling and enjoying the visit but me, well, not so much. Nevertheless, we truly could not believe what we were witnessing.

Someone or something was getting pissed off now and telling me, "Enough is enough with the self-doubt, Ray!" Suddenly, it stopped as quickly as it had appeared. Neither one of us spoke a fucking word. We just sat there completely stunned for several minutes holding each other on the bench in front of the unlit fire pit overlooking the beautiful lake in the distance. They were really not accepting my self-doubt any longer. Neither was Jessica. It was time I stepped up and used this ability for someone or something.

Chapter 21:

Breakthroughs in Arkansas

Medium Bonnie invited Jessica and I to a retreat in Arkansas to practice and learn techniques in the dome owned by one of her friends. Her friend is one of the most amazing and inspiring people I've ever met. She lost one of her children in a boating accident. The story brought us to tears, but she uses this horrific occurrence to fuel her drive and determination to help other people—people like me, a very confused man, who lacked spirituality and faith in anything.

In the four days I spent with them, this woman had a huge impact on my life. She showed me how to take all the bad shit life throws at you and use it to make something beautiful. When I was debating whether to write this book, her story gave me the motivation and courage to put myself out there, to possibly help someone else and pay it forward.

I hope one day you get to the Hot Springs area of Arkansas, and visit the dome. It is a magical experience. You will come home a different person. A better version of yourself.

When we first arrived at the retreat, (there were about fifteen of us or so) we all chose a random folder. Inside each folder was a quote. Mine read, "I have learned more from my pain than I ever learned from my pleasure." I knew at that moment I was in the right place—the place I needed to be.

"Training" (Journal Entry—Fall, 2019)

I was in the Hot Springs area in Arkansas with Jessica and Medium Bonnie at a retreat designed to explore my abilities and learn to use them with confidence. A group of about twelve of us gathered for a four-day event of intense training and exercises. For our first exercise, we were asked to meditate and connect with our guides while we were there. It took a little while for me to get connected, but I managed to eventually. I was met by a panel of three guides who seemed preoccupied with something other than me. I needed to stay present, so I asked them if I could stay. At first, I was ignored, so I asked again and then again. They were not overly interested that I was at a retreat and really needed to connect with them, but they eventually allowed it. I was not permitted to ask anything of them or be given anything, so I just stayed silent and watched while they worked on something. My physical body was in a meditative state at this time.

The last two times I connected with my guides, there were seven of them, not just three, and not the usual ones either. I "see" them in my mind's eye as a bunch of lines that are black, white, silver, and some gold around the outside. They always appear this way to me. I can identify my guides by these colors of lines grouped together.

My interpretation of this is that I can connect to my guides if I want to at will, but that does not mean I will be able to ask them to give me advice or listen to me. They can also push me aside very easily if they want to. Guides and masters have much power. I feel like some of them like me more than others. A very strange feeling to get from someone who isn't part of my realm of existence per se, but I guess they aren't much different from the human beings walking the Earth in that regard.

After the first day of the retreat, Jessica and I returned to the hotel to get some sleep. We were both pretty exhausted from the day's activities. Believe it or not, entering other realms and giving and receiving telepathic messages is completely exhausting. As someone who exercises almost every day, I can tell you that connecting universally is more stressful on the body than working out. Perhaps it is because I am new at it.

As soon as I got undressed and got into bed, I was instantly greeted by a room full of energies. I am not sure why it came as such a surprise. Imagine yourself on the other side, hoping to communicate with our world and a handful of people who can actually do this all get together in the same place. Word apparently got out up there, and they flocked to my hotel room. Others in our group said the following day that they had experienced a similar thing.

When Jessica got into bed, I said, "Do you see or feel them?"

She said, "Is the room full again?"

"Yep."

"What are you going to do?" she asked. "Tell them to come back tomorrow."

"Hey everyone, call me tomorrow!" I said.

Some remained persistent, so I said to them again, "I am going to sleep. If you want to hang around and watch me, fine, but I am going to sleep."

Something happened that night, and I am still trying to figure out if it was real. I felt someone or something grab my right ankle. Jessica was sleeping on my left side, so there was no chance it was her. It woke me up and scared the shit out of me. I was not sure if I was dreaming this or not because I was very tired, but either way, I was pissed off and screamed (inside my head of course), "Touch me again, I will fucking kill you!"

Yeah, yeah, I know what you are going to say. It isn't a particularly great idea to threaten a dead person with death, but if it was real, it stopped and didn't happen again. I think I got my point across, even though my choice of wording could perhaps have been better.

"The Warrior" (Journal Entry—Fall, 2019)

At this point, I am still undecided about whether we have past lives. There is actually a lot of evidence to support that there is. Brian L. Weiss wrote a great book on the subject called *Many Lives, Many Masters*, which I highly recommend reading if you want to learn more about his research on past lives.

What I don't understand, however, is why. What is the purpose of us returning repeatedly? Also, I doubt we are the only intelligent life form in the entire universe, so wouldn't it be conceivable that if we did come back one or more of those times, we would have lived on another planet in a different life form?

Let's go back to the dome in Arkansas. One of the last things we did was explore past life regressions. The entire group, with Jessica and me included, were hypnotized and asked to go back into our past lives and bring them to the forefront of our minds. When we awoke, some folks shared their stories with the group.

This is an excerpt from Jessica's journal. This is what she saw while hypnotized at the dome and her description of her past life regression.

My first vision: Jesus on the cross. It's far away. I walk closer to it, and I am in a church. I am alone. I am looking around. The church is empty. I am in Greece, and my name is Andromeda. It's the Middle Ages, I think. I have long blond hair, which is pulled back in a long ponytail with three different hair bands sectioning it off down my back. I'm wearing a fitted white gown with gold trim. I am happy. I come there to feed poor children from the village. They come to the church and I give them food, coins, whatever I can. This brings me much happiness.

My second vision: I am on a boat with big sails. I am alone. It is daytime, and I am sailing a big boat by myself. I love it. I am probably not supposed to be doing this; my parents will be upset with me, but not too much. I am a bit of a rebel spirit, and I love the water. I love being on boats and fishing and doing things of that nature. I am at peace on the water and on my boat. I am happy. Even in my current life, the water is everything to me. I need it to feel recharged, to feel peace, to feel centered, and to feel energized.

My third vision: It is nighttime, and I am sitting under a big beautiful tree. There is a huge, full moon showing behind the branches of the tree. I am lonely. I am not sad, but I am lonely. I love my life, I know I am lucky and privileged, but I feel lonely. I see big wooden wagon wheels; chariots or horse-drawn carriages are going by. I do not know what or who they are, but they are heading toward my village. My love is on one of those chariots. I do not see him, I never do, but I know he is heading to my village and that I will meet him there.

Lastly, my death: I am in my bed, in my home. I am old, and I am surrounded by my family: children, cousins, others who love me. I am not sad; I am ready. I have lived a long and fulfilling life. I have been blessed and lucky. I am grateful. My beloved has gone before me; I do not know how, but he is already gone. I am going to see him now. My father (in this lifetime) is there, but he is not my father; he is my brother or cousin or something. He is by me as I die. It is peaceful.

I ascend in an amazing swirl of lights and colors. I see a book, but I have so many words and sayings swirling around my head, I am not certain I will get any ascertainable message out of all of it. I open the book and everything else stops. The words jump off of the page at me: "Your life is everything. Do something with your gifts."

My loved ones, higher spirits, spirit guides, masters, all come to me. It looks like a million points of light in all different primary colors. I have never seen anything like this before in any of my meditations. It reminds me of snow from an old school TV when the station has gone offline, except it is not black and white; it is vibrant and colorful and warm and euphoric. My father and grandfather are there, and they are hugging me, and the points of light became even more intense. It was one of the most beautiful moments of my life.

Later that night, I shared this with Ray. I had just figured he had no recollection of his own regression because he hadn't said anything about it the entire day or night.

At dinner, I began to tell him about my regression and about midway through, he stopped me and said, "I was a guard for the Emperor of the Eastern Roman Empire in the 1400s."

I'm like, "Yeah, but I was in Greece."

I admit, I really remember nothing from my history classes and I was like, "Why are you telling me this?" and he said, "Because Greece was a part of the Eastern Roman Empire in the 1400s, and I was on that chariot. I was a soldier and guard to the Emperor. But just as we got to that point of the hypnosis, I passed out and fell asleep."

I actually remember that part of the session because Ray began snoring in the middle of the dome. We laughed so hard. Honestly, I have no idea if that timeline pans out or if it even matters because all things are happening at once, but regardless, we thought it was really cool.

Souls find each other from one life to the next. What is better than that?

I remember clearly during my own hypnosis being on that chariot. Medium Bonnie has also told me I was a warrior in multiple past lives. In fact, that is the nickname she has given me. I have had many times in my present life where I have had the ability to fight, defend, or protect without even thinking of what to do or how to do it. Could that be from a past life? I am really uncertain whether past lives happen to exist, but the evidence is mounting in favor of its reality at this point.

It certainly feels like I knew Jessica before this life as well. We have always had an unusual amount of "déjà vu" moments. One day, she and I were talking after a romantic evening in the gazebo in the backyard, and I said to her, "I always felt I would kill for you. Perhaps I already have."

"To Share" (Journal Entry—Fall, 2019)

Still at the retreat, we were asked to connect with our guides and get two words to describe what we must do in this life. My answer was very vivid and clear: "to share." Jessica's was also vivid and clear: "to show."

When we all awakened from our meditation, we were each asked if we wanted to tell everyone our two words. Jessica went first with her "to show." When she said those words, I was blown away, and she saw the look on my face. Everyone in the room was touched by her experience. Then it was my turn to share my two words, and when I said they were "to share," Jessica was dumbfounded. We were both just stunned. Could two people on this Earth possibly be any more meant for each other than she and I?

The second thing we were told to ask for was one word to describe who or what we are. Mine again was very clear. The word was "warrior," which Medium Bonnie had told me before. She got this from her guides at our first meeting, so this description wasn't a surprise to me.

The third thing we were asked to do was to think consciously of what best described what we wanted to do to improve ourselves. This is what I wrote: "Continue to grow, learn, and love. Learn as much as I can. Grow into something better, and love the people I love with everything I am." Then I had to give those written words to my partner Jessica, who was instructed to reduce the sentences to just three words and focus on those three words through her own meditation. During this extremely intense meditation, Jessica was to create a ball of energy, and when she said so, "push" that ball of energy with those words into my head, or my third eye, as it is called.

I remember feeling unworthy of receiving anything from Jessica. This isn't unusual for me. I have had to go out and earn all that I have and all that I am. I have never been just given anything. Therefore, when anyone is giving me something, I feel as though I have not earned it, and therefore, I am unworthy of receiving it.

I remember my head shaking, as if I were saying no, just before the ball was pushed into me. I needed to be able to receive, especially from Jessica.

I then had to give Jessica her ball with the three words I'd chosen from her writings. I really put my all into this. I went into a deep state of meditation. A few times, I felt I was losing some momentum. I recall screaming to the universe, "Get your shit together! Let's go! It's now or never. Don't let me down." I was trying to hold the ball together with everything I had. Every little ounce of energy in my entire being was inside that ball. When she said to release it, I pushed it into Jessica's third eye with everything I had.

The universe didn't let me down, but it certainly didn't make it easy for me. The result, according to Jessica, was a most amazing transference of energy from me to her that had her feeling completely uplifted and euphoric. I remember looking at her then and seeing that she was the happiest I had ever seen her in all our time together. I was completely exhausted to the point of barely being able to stand up afterward, but it was worth it, and I would do it again and again for her.

My interpretation of this experience is that, firstly, I must "share" my story with others. I feel the need to help those who want to develop their abilities. That is part of my objective with this book and perhaps more books to come. Secondly, I am a warrior who can overcome almost anything in my life, and thirdly, I must be open to receiving things given to me that come from love or a good place, especially from good people.

"The Circle of Fear" (Journal Entry—Fall, 2019)

The most difficult thing that was asked of me came as an exercise on the last day. First, on arriving at the dome in the morning, we saw a setup like no other we had seen yet. In the very center of the dome on the floor was a group of pillows with this large red one in the center. It almost looked like a throne for a king. A throne of pillows. All around them were smaller pillows for each of us in the group to sit on, making a circle around the throne. Oh shit, I thought. Someone was going to sit in the middle on the throne, and I already knew that that someone was going to be me.

Since I'd arrived at the dome, I'd had a considerably difficult time "sharing" anything with anyone. I barely believed in this stuff myself at this point and so sharing it as though it was fact or to speak about myself in this context was quite difficult.

I remember at the end of the second day in the dome, I had opened up a little and shared a few of my experiences with some of the folks who were present. They were completely fascinated and intrigued by some of my experiences and would ask me questions about my past events, even though I could barely explain any of this because I was still learning about it myself. Someone said something about my sacral chakra.

"What the hell is that?" I said. "Hey Jessica, is this woman talking about my dick?"

I really was a newbie at this point, but that only seemed to cause more intrigue among the other attendees, who asked question after question about how my process worked, what I saw, and how I saw it. I was becoming increasingly self-conscious. I felt like a freak. One woman who was very nice kept asking me questions about my near-death experience. I answered several of them and stated that I really did not talk about it very much. She asked why and I said "because it's hard answering all the questions people ask without getting emotional." She said, "Oh, I am so sorry to be asking you all of this, but can I just ask you one more question please?"

Ugh!

Now I was going to be thrown in the center of this whole thing and get picked apart. Medium Bonnie had been trying to get me to open up more the whole time I was there. She felt this was for my own benefit, of course. Upon walking into the dome that day, she was already in the middle of addressing the entire group to get us mentally prepared for what was coming next.

As Jessica and I were walking in and heading to our places, Medium Bonnie went on to say, "What are you guys here for anyway? You all must participate and give this everything you've got! Are you here to make progress and learn about yourself, or are you going to quit when it gets a little tough? Are you a 'warrior' or not? Are you here 'to share' yourself or run away from yourself?" Although she was addressing the entire group, I think everyone in that dome knew exactly who she was really speaking to in that moment. Now that I was called out, I just had to step up.

Here was the next exercise on her agenda.

"Someone is going to sit in the middle of this room. Everyone else will sit around the circle and yell out the experiences they can extract from your conscious mind using only their abilities. You must be completely open and honest with all of us if you agree to sit in the center seat. This will be difficult for many of you to do. I understand if you are apprehensive, but if you agree to do it, you must go all in."

She was looking at me as she spoke. It's now or never, I thought. If I don't do this, I will regret it forever. I have to be in that seat. As I was literally trying to convince myself to do it I rose up off my pillow and said, "Okay, Bonnie, I'll do it."

I walked to the center, sat in the pillow throne, and closed my eyes. I never opened my eyes while I was there in the center. Medium Bonnie gave everyone their instructions. This was no holds barred. Anyone could talk about any of my shit and, oh boy, did I have a lot of shit!

"The person in the center will hear from each person in the room. That person in the center may answer three ways: 'Thank you,' 'That is interesting,' or 'I will need to think about that further.' This is so no one's feelings are hurt by potentially being wrong." I didn't want anyone to be wrong. I really didn't, so what I tried to do was think really hard about the various life experiences and push them to the forefront of my mind to make this easier for a fellow psychic to extract. I could also control some of what was going to be said by doing this.

I don't remember all of them, but here are some of the significant hits, and there were many.

Someone mentioned my cat that had died. I was really broken up about losing that cat because she was my first validation that I wasn't crazy when you think about it. She could see the things I could see and sense the energies in the room with me.

Someone said crayon. I really didn't want that one to come out, but the crayon incident from an earlier chapter of this book was out there now.

Someone said fire. I kind of served that one up on a platter. Of course, it referred to my near-death experience. This was getting very difficult to talk about, but I tried to keep my composure and continue on. By now, there wasn't a dry eye in the place. I could hear the other attendees sobbing and blowing their nose.

Someone said bullet and that quickly followed up with wounded. I had been shot at in the past and another time had a gun held up to my head. I could feel the cold steel of the weapon right behind my ear. My past traumas were coming out now, and this was proving to be so fucking difficult that I began to rock back and forth. I tried to enter a meditative state while talking about the most personal details of my life.

Then Jessica said, "Forest."

I said, "I need more."

She said, "Go through it," and I replied, "I will."

This proved to be an interesting statement later on. This would become a repetitive mantra that we would begin to see everywhere.

When the exercise ended, I would love to tell you that I came out of that circle feeling great, but the fact is I didn't. It may have given me the courage to write this book, however, and open up about these past experiences. I certainly felt the emotion in that room. A room filled with many pure souls that seemed to care for me—people I previously thought would never have allowed me to be a part of their world. My soul was far from pure.

I do hope I helped the other people there, even if only in some small way. They certainly helped me a lot. Many thanked me at the end for sharing, and I thanked them in return. I think each person took something different away from that experience, myself included. I had much to work on myself. It was time to begin.

The Forest; the only way out is through.

Part III
The Science—"The Afterlife"

CHAPTER 22:

Quantum Consciousness

The first law of thermodynamics, also known as the Law of Conservation of Energy, states that energy can neither be created nor destroyed; energy can only be transferred or changed from one form to another.

Therefore, all energy is renewable in the sense that all energy will be altered or broken down and then changed into some other form of energy. The energy is then transferred to something else that has energy. This energy is not limited to the sun, coal, gas, oil, and the like; this includes human energy. That is, the thoughts, feelings, words, and things that make up our conscious state of being are also made up of energy.

Quantum physics tells us that there is no such thing as "empty space." Even in space, or the void, there are particles of matter and antimatter that cancel each other out instantly. These particles aren't visible to the eye, but we know they are there. It is this concept that explains how the universe came to be. With that much energy in these tiny spaces that can result in the creation of a universe (i.e., the Big Bang Theory), is it that difficult to believe that there is unlimited potential or energy within space that a person could tap into and utilize? We know that "dark energy" and "dark matter" exist in what we thought at one time to be void. We now know that there is something where we once thought there was absolutely nothing.

In physical cosmology and astronomy, dark energy is an unknown form of energy, which is hypothesized to permeate all of space, tending to accelerate the expansion of the universe. Einstein discovered the expansion in what we once thought was a stagnant universe, but he was unable to prove this theory until the great scientist Edwin Hubble was able to verify that the universe is not only expanding, but it is doing so at a much more rapid pace than we ever thought. Another part of Hubble's discovery is that we are not the only galaxy out there in space. In fact, there are more galaxies than we can possibly count.

So, what is fueling the growth and rapid expansion of these galaxies? The quick answer is dark energy. This is not my discovery by any means. This has been scientifically proven by the world's greatest scholars and scientists.

One of the other important scientific discoveries that puzzles the great minds of the world is that as the universe expands, its density doesn't seem to change. How can this be? If dark energy is expanding the universe, then it only makes sense that the density of space will change as the expansion occurs. My theory explains why the density remains relatively constant.

Dark matter is thought to account for approximately eighty-five percent of all matter in the universe and about a quarter of its total energy density. The majority of dark matter is thought to be non-baryonic in nature, possibly composed of some as-yet undiscovered subatomic particles. Let's put dark matter aside for now and focus more on dark energy.

We know that every atom is made of protons, neutrons, electrons, a nucleus (the center), and space. Invisible "space" exists in every atom of every cell in the universe. More of this "space" exists than does solid matter.

These electrons in the atoms jump from one rotation around its nucleus to another. This phenomenon is called a "quantum leap." A quantum leap is a discontinuous transition between quantum states. What this means is that an electron in one energy level in an atom jumps instantly into another energy level, emitting or absorbing energy as it does so. There is no in-between state, and it doesn't take any time for the leap to occur.

Therefore, there must be energy stored within every atom in every cell to have any such movement at all. All matter, including dark matter, contains energy. Hence, there is energy in all spaces, including what we thought were voids. We know it is there, but we cannot see it with our eyes. We can't seem to pick it up with any of our natural human senses. Or can we?

CHAPTER 23:

Scientific Proof That There Is Energy Everywhere—What Does This Mean?

This scientific proof means that all energy is passed on. It never goes away completely. For example, when you eat an apple, the apple is broken down by your digestive system and converted into energy. You then use that energy to, let's say, play the piano. The piano passes the energy into sound waves. The sound waves travel to someone's ear. When they listen to the music, it makes them want to dance. Why would music make someone want to dance or move? Because sound waves have energy. The energy is continuously transformed and passed on to someone or something else. We say that the energy can be used up, but really, it is only passed on from one form to another and then another infinitely.

Information also contains energy. For example, if you close your eyes and I stand behind you and snap my fingers, you hear a click. Furthermore, you know the click came from behind you, but how do you know that? Only your eyes can really tell you where something is by looking at it. So, then, how do you know where the sound waves of that click are coming from? Your ears cannot directly give you this information unless it is embedded in the sound waves. Therefore, the sound waves enter your ears carrying information that tells you it is coming from behind you. Information is therefore a form of energy.

The snap of my fingers came from my human physical energy, which was transformed and transmitted through sound waves to your ears, but to know where that energy came from without sight, there must be something else in the sound wave that your mind can decode.

Do you need more examples that information contains, or better yet, *is* energy? Have you ever read a book that inspired you to do something? Have you seen a movie that made you cry? Has a motivational speaker ever gotten you jumping up and down? His words contain energy. They were converted to sound waves, which is energy. It made you react physically in some way shape or form. You went out and started a business after hearing him. One simple online business that delivers one billion products to people overnight annually through your information-based website, which makes people want to order stuff from you. You are the wealthiest person in the world. How am I doing so far? Information is energy!

CHAPTER 24:

My Theory

Okay. I am about to give you my theory of life, death, consciousness, transference of thoughts as energy, and the afterlife. This is *my* theory. I am not a scientist. I am not an astronomer or a physicist, although I loved the little bit of physics I learned in school while all of my schoolmates hated them. I don't know how to go about doing it, but I would love to one day work with scientists who are willing to help me prove this theory.

My theory on why the universe continues to expand is that we continually dump more dark energy into space or into the so-called void. Where does this dark energy come from that we can't see but we know is there, and why is more of it being continuously dumped into the void or space between all things?

Could it be that the energy within our consciousness needs a place to go when our body dies? If you subscribe to the theory that all energy is transferable and that the conscious mind is made up of energy, then that energy must go somewhere. This would also explain why the density of the universe is a constant and why the universe is expanding so rapidly. More people equal more deaths. More deaths mean that more dark energy is released into the void.

If information can be extracted from energy and picked up by the human brain in this way, then it is possible to transmit information to one another using nothing more than energy—energy that the human body and, more importantly, the human mind produces. One can release information into the "void" (which we already know isn't really a void) or space in between all things, and that information can be carried through by dark matter or dark energy to another human brain, another living organism, or another energy-based being. The things you say and do that you put out there into the universe can be picked up on by other energy-carrying entities, such as living things, and can be reacted to by those living things. Very few people consciously possess the ability to interpret these thoughts and energy, make sense of it, and then explain it or deliver it to someone else. These are the people who are said to have ESP, or extrasensory perception. Some refer to it as a "sixth sense" or a form of telepathy. It is my belief that we all have this ability within us, but some can utilize it, recognize it, and perhaps even invoke it better than others.

When we die, what happens to our energy? Our human energy is tied directly to our conscious mind. Where does this go? Energy doesn't cease to exist. It is transformative. This we already know. So, it must go somewhere. My theory is that we become part of the universal dark energy. We become part of something much greater than ourselves—the entire universe in fact. We become limitless with our conscious minds—a part of a cosmic and universal collective consciousness, if you will. We become part of the universe's energy structure, forever expanding it.

I believe dark energy is the energy extracted from the conscious mind when the body dies.

This is why I feel that science and religion can coexist. It's because of what I refer to as "The Energetic Consciousness", the church would call spirits or souls. Read on; we have only just scratched the surface!

At this point, you may wish to invoke your personal religious beliefs as to where you are, where you may be after death, and whether you will reincarnate, etc., but for now, if you can imagine this is the starting point for the afterlife and whatever comes next, you will be able to digest and accept my theory regardless of your personal religion or even if you have no religious beliefs at all. Religion and science can coexist in harmony, at least in my theory they can if you want them to.

So when you are sitting around and you get a "telepathic message" from somewhere, but you have no idea where it came from or why you received it, could it simply be that it was passed to you through a dark energy-based being or as part of the universal consciousness? It is important to understand that scientists call it dark energy because it cannot be seen with the naked eye and not because it is dark in an evil sense of the word.

Has anyone ever said to you something like, "Do not say that out loud; it will come true" or "Don't even put that thought out there? Don't even say it"?

Think about that. Does information contain energy? Does it have power? Is energy transferable? Is it so impossible to believe that you may be able to pick up on, take in, and decode energy that contains information? Doesn't your mobile phone act in a similar manner? Is there any electronic device that is more advanced than the human mind?

It may be a rare ability to consciously possess and accept information this way, but subconsciously, it is happening to you all the time. I find that more and more people are beginning to recognize that they have this ability, and as we continue to evolve, it will become easier to recognize in each future generation.

Chapter 25:

What's on the Other Side?

"The other side" refers to realms of existence where the energy that once existed in your conscious mind continues to exist in another form that we as humans cannot see, touch, hear, or smell. As I stated previously, I believe that this is what scientists refer to as "dark energy." This is the energy source that continues to force our universe to expand instead of contract. In most religions, this is called your spirit or soul. As I am trying to remain more on the scientific side of things, I will call them "energy beings."

The realm where we exist immediately upon our death may not be the only other realm of existence. There may be several other realms. I also believe that the energy beings that exist in other realms do so in some form of a hierarchy or structure. The different levels are perhaps based on their abilities and experiences. Immediately upon death, we will exist in what some folks call the fourth realm or fourth dimension. I do not like to use the word dimension because I feel a better term is realm. Let's use the word realm for now. This realm, entered immediately upon death, is a transitional state of being—a first stop, if you will. This is where I think Jessica's dad is currently. He is staying there by choice because he has unfinished business here on Earth. I have no doubt he can "move up" the hierarchy, so to speak, but I think he may lose the ability to interact with his family and those close to his family, like me, if he does. Therefore, he chooses not to. This realm allows those in it to be closer to us living beings. However, it is just as difficult for them to communicate with us as it is for us to communicate with them. When Jessica's dad found me, he was thrilled because he knew I could "hear" him.

In this realm, energy beings can appear to you and me on what looks like a movie screen in your mind. They can present themselves in any version of themselves they wish. The first time I met Jessica's dad, I had no idea it was him because in the photo I had seen, he was lighter and had shaved his beard. I believe that the dead in the fourth realm can appear to me in the form of their choosing, meaning they can present themselves as a younger or older version of themselves. Jessica's dad also chose to appear to me in the shirt he wore on the Christmas Eve before he died. I think this was so Jessica could easily identify that it was him by my description; they will also use other identifiers as needed. If you recall, the one man told me that if his wife didn't believe me to just remind her of the silly shoes he once wore. The reminder of the silly shoes gave her a laugh and validation at the same time.

There are no other realms where I can see a person the way they looked here on Earth. In other higher levels of the hierarchy, I cannot envision them as having any physical form but only as lines that are black, white, silver, and gold. The lines are always moving slightly. I cannot tell a male from a female. It's quite possible they are no longer either because they are now a part of the universe's energy structure. They have much more power and can pass on to me a euphoric feeling through vibrations in my body. They are who I refer to as guides and masters. These are energy beings who choose to help or "guide" people or perhaps other energy beings in their realm as well. There are various levels of masters. In my next account ("There the Whole Time"), I tell you about how I once met one of my guides. I could barely see him, and it took a long while for me to realize he was there. We couldn't, or perhaps just didn't, connect right away. It's unfortunate it took as long as it did for me to find him. He is extremely important to the writing of this book. He is the one who gave me my future life's path and directed me toward what I needed to do, or what I "must" do, I should say. Therefore, to me, he is most important. I now visit and commutate back and forth with him regularly.

I previously told you about a panel of three masters I met. They were stronger in the sense that they could actually transfer energy to me to use here on Earth or pass it to Jessica or others. At the retreat, while at the dome in Arkansas, the panel of three masters was with me all the time. They helped me learn by giving me significant breakthroughs in my abilities. They were easy to connect with during this time and I felt they had significantly more power.

Another level up in the hierarchy are the masters I told you about in a previous chapter. They are a panel of seven, and they are so strong and powerful that they gave me an out-of-body experience where I may have been one of those "speeding lines" in someone else's universe or realm. I could fly around at the speed of the light in that realm. They allowed me to return and then come back at will. They gave me total control of my experience. Before the experience began, my room was filled with the most amazing feelings of energy, and I had an actual audience of other energy beings. I remember asking my teacher, why the others were there observing. She said, "Maybe they were all rooting for you and wanted you to succeed."

At the time of this occurrence, I was completely petrified by all of this happening to me, but later, all I could think was, Please, let me come back and do it again. It has never again happened since that day, unfortunately. Their power is most intense, and their capabilities are simply incredible.

At the top of the hierarchy (or the highest level I have ever been or seen) is the all-powerful, all-knowing, and extremely loving divine energy. He carries with him the light. There is never much light behind him, as he seems to be the source of the light or have the ability to direct it. Some of my teachers have referred to him as Jesus, and that may be so. I have been told by other mediums that Jesus is with me often. Now, whether they actually mean Jesus as a metaphorical figure for the divine celestial being he is or whether it really is Jesus, I don't claim to know, but I am truly honored and grateful each and any time I am allowed in his presence.

I recall the last time he visited me. I was very confused and in a bad place. I just couldn't make sense of all that was happening to me, and I was going on and on about my troubles. He listened. The visit was just a few seconds, but a lot can happen in a split second in other realms, especially with someone like him. Anyway, he had to go, and again—without him saying anything—he began to leave and all my troubles seemed to become small and trivial. A feeling of peace and calm overtook my body. I thanked him, and he was gone. Gone also were my feelings of anxiety, fear, and lack of confidence. He never speaks; he doesn't need to, and he doesn't stay long because he doesn't have to. When he leaves me, I feel amazing, and I just know what I must do next. My problem is solved, my anxiety gone, and my faith restored.

"There the Whole Time" (Journal Entry—Winter, 2019)

It was December 26, 2019. Jessica and I decided to go to Florida for a few days. I slept at her house the night before we left because our flight was very early in the morning. I was lying in bed. Jessica had more things to pack, so I told her I would meditate while she finished getting ready.

She said, "Won't I bother you?"

"No, my love."

I went into my meditation, entered another realm, and looked for my guides. They do not resemble any human form, so they can sort of blend into other things and be hard to view. I had been unable to reach any of my guides in a while, and I was getting frustrated. Jessica and I were planning big changes in our lives, and I needed advice. I rarely ask them for anything for myself. I was about to give up and come out of the meditation when something moved into the lower right-hand side of my view. There were some black lines, with a little white and silver mixed in. That is a guide! How is it I never saw him before? I had seen this guide before but never realized what he was. Holy shit! I must have gone past him nearly fifty times before.

He seemed a little pissed off and I suppose rightfully so. He must have thought I was looking for someone else to talk to, but he had been right there the whole time. I explained that I simply hadn't noticed him before. He was sitting sideways to me. (Okay, now you are thinking how do I possibly know he was sitting sideways if he has no human form? The answer is I have no fucking idea. I just know. It's the same way I know

144

if they turn and look away from me, even though they have no head. I just know.)

Anyway, he turned and faced me as I asked what I had come to ask: "What do I need to do?" In my left hand appeared a blank letter-sized white piece of paper. I stared at the paper and said, "I don't understand." Then a blue pen appeared in my right hand. He said "Write," and with that he disappeared. I asked him to wait, but he didn't. I apologized repeatedly after he was gone for not noticing him sooner, but I didn't know if he knew how sorry I was. I thanked him for the information. I had so many doubts about writing this book. Now I knew it was something I had to do.

Before I exited the meditation, I saw one more thing. I saw a US soldier on one knee in great pain with his head down. I didn't know what to make of this until I got to Florida. One day at the resort, I entered the bathroom by the swimming pool. The only other man inside was wearing swim trunks without a shirt, and I could see a scar from a large bullet hole on his back. I waited for him to turn around, and I saw the exit wound on his abdomen. I simply thanked him for his service. I have so much respect for the men and women who defend our country. I only wish I knew what I was supposed to do, but perhaps that was it. Perhaps on that day I was supposed to let him know he was appreciated. Maybe no one had thanked him for taking that bullet for us.

My interpretation was that I must write this book. I'm not sure why or what will come of it. I don't know if I am writing it for myself or for others. I just know that this is what I have to do. I must complete this book.

"The Haunting" (Journal Entry—Winter, 2019)

Still in Florida, Jessica and I arrived at our hotel and checked in. It was quite nice. We unpacked and relaxed. Jessica left the room and I was watching TV waiting for her to return. I heard *ZZZZ, ZZZZ, ZZZZ.* Three times. I looked around but ignored it. Since I have had this happen in other hotels so many times, I already knew what it was. Besides, I could feel the presence in the room. Later that night, Jessica and I were about to go to sleep. She fell asleep first, and as I got up to use the bathroom, I heard *ZZZZ, ZZZZ, ZZZZ*, three more times. The next day it happened one more time and then I closed my eyes briefly and told whatever it was, "If you wanted to talk to me, you went about it all wrong. Fuck you, now! You shouldn't have tried to scare the shit out of us in the middle of the night." There were no more noises for the rest of the week.

"My Aching Head" (Journal Entry—Winter, 2019)

It was December 27, 2019. I had a realization. When there is another person in the room or my immediate area who has a very strong connection to the afterlife, I sometimes know instantly. In some cases, it can be a very uncomfortable feeling. I wonder why it is this way with some and yet with others I can be attracted to their ability. It is almost like when two magnets of the same north or south pole try to touch one another they can't; they just repel one another. But if one is north and one is south, they connect and stick together instantly. I do not know why this happens with certain people and not others. It isn't the normal negative gut feeling either. It actually becomes physical in nature.

We were still in Florida, and Jessica and I were sitting at a swimming pool at the hotel. The woman who was sitting on the other side of me had an intensity that was so strong that it was hurting my head, and I'm sure I was hurting hers. She kept looking over at me, and I could see in her face that she was becoming increasingly more uncomfortable. She would speak to her husband and then look over at Jessica and me. At one point, she held her head and said to her husband, "Let's go."

One of us had to leave that pool.

She left. I wasn't giving in to the extreme headache—and besides, I'd only just arrived at the pool, and she had been there for a while. Neither of us spoke a word about it, not knowing if the other believed in anything. Like I have said before, this is a terrible conversation starter.

"Can You Feel Me?" (Journal Entry—Winter, 2019)

The following day, December 28, 2019, Jessica was upset about something. I wanted her to feel better and to know how much I loved her. It was a beautiful night in Florida, so I suggested we meditate. She was lying next to me in bed, and I placed my right hand over her heart. My left was above her head with the palm up, and I began to go into a very deep and intense trance-like state, summoning my guides to help me help her. At about five minutes in, nothing was happening, and I was about to give up. Then her legs began to twitch. They started going faster and faster until she was kicking frantically, as though she was running. This lasted for only about twenty seconds or so. Afterward, I just held her and lay with her. She got up, went to the bathroom, and came back to bed with no recollection of her legs shaking. She said she did feel better, though. Sometimes when we have severe blockages in the energy flow of our bodies and they are suddenly released, the result can be a trembling or shaking in the extremities. Similar to what I experienced with Nicole at the beginning of this book.

CHAPTER 26:

Spooky Action at a Distance—Albert Einstein

"Spooky action at a distance": This is how Albert Einstein referred to quantum entanglement when it was first presented to him. I know what you're thinking. "More physics?" Yes, more physics. Let me reiterate my position on all things. I don't believe in anything until I can justify it through science. I was my own biggest skeptic. I tore apart everything that was happening to me and broke it down into small bits and pieces that were explainable by the laws of physics. Until it was explainable by science, I believed it was nonsense, as did Albert Einstein at first.

Quantum entanglement is a physical phenomenon that occurs when pairs or groups of particles are generated, interact, or share spatial proximity (i.e., get entangled) in such ways that the quantum state of each particle cannot be described independently of the state of the others, even when the particles are separated by a large distance.

Let me see if I can give you a less scientific definition. In quantum physics, entangled particles remain connected so that actions performed on one affect the other, even when separated by great distances. This is quite important to understand because what we are saying here is that one particle, say in New York, can affect another particle in Los Angeles at the exact same time. What must travel from one particle to the other to tell it that it is time to make a change? Energy—yes, energy! It also must travel faster than the speed of light, and for that reason Einstein didn't like the concept because he felt that the speed of light was the fastest anything could travel.

So if one energetic particle can affect another energetic particle, is it now that hard to believe that one's consciousness in one part of the world can affect another person's consciousness in another part? I'll leave that for you to decide, but I now believe it can. I also believe that when it comes to consciousness, if both parties know each other, either party can make the connection, and it becomes somewhat easier. Also, if they are thinking of each other, it becomes easier still. If someone is thinking about me, and I then focus on them, it is far easier to make the connection happen. How many times have you thought of someone out of the blue and they called you on the phone? If one practices this enough, I do believe you can pretty much tap into anyone. A third party can be used as a conduit or connector. This is why you are able to ask a medium about a deceased loved one. The connection goes from you to the loved one, through the medium first, and then information from the other side comes back through the medium to you.

This, in essence, was the beginning of my journey. I was being "hit" by others' consciousness and didn't know what was happening. How could I know the things I knew about people without ever speaking to them? In the beginning, I just assumed these were things that I had heard before, stored in my memory somewhere, and then retrieved when I needed them. Perhaps I'd watched a video, visited their website, or met one of their friends. Over time, however, I found that I knew really private things about certain people that would never have been posted on the Internet or said by a third party. It just became too much to deny any longer.

"Give It to Me Straight" (Journal Entry—Summer, 2019)

I felt a message coming through for a day and a half with the usual chest pains. Very strong, shaky, low vibrations. Very annoying. I could tell it would be either bad or serious news. Later that night, with Jessica by my side, I requested the message to come through. Jessica often gives me the courage to do these things that I am really uncomfortable about.

This was early on in my progress, and one of the first times I had ever requested a message be delivered to me. I began to meditate and asked Jessica's dad or anyone listening in the universe to give me the message. In the vision, I saw two people, we both knew. One was quite angry with the other and was pointing a finger in the face of the other with a look of extreme anger. This meant nothing to us at the time. I asked if Jessica knew any reason why these two particular folks would argue. She said that would be completely out of character for either of them.

The next day, more of the vision came through to me. Sometimes, the original message is fragmented but will come forward later and be more vivid and clear. One person was warning the other of something serious in nature. I called Jessica to tell her the rest of what I'd seen.

Before I shared the rest of the message with Jessica, she told me that a fight had indeed occurred between the two of them shortly after I'd told her I had seen one. I insisted that she didn't tell me what the argument was about until I told her what the rest of the vision was so as to check my accuracy. As I respect and want to maintain their privacy, I can only tell you I was accurate.

Jessica's dad continues to give me information with extreme precision, at times making it impossible to deny the reality of what is happening. This especially when it pertains to his daughter or his family.

CHAPTER 27:

Why We Don't Have a Clear Conscience When It Comes to Consciousness

Very early in the 1500s, science speculated that we have six senses, not five, the sixth being our consciousness. As consciousness was increasingly explored, it seemed to be somewhat at odds with the church and what the church referred to as spirituality. During this period, the church was all knowing and all powerful. Therefore, science and the church basically made a deal with each other, stating that science would stay out of spirituality and that the church would stay out of science. If any scientist did not adhere to these rules, the church would condemn them to death. This practice of killing people who explored consciousness as a sixth sense or who went against the church's ruling extended all the way into the 1800s. They would be labeled a heretic or a witch and burned. Three hundred years of killing people made a very clear statement and basically stifled most research on the topic.

For hundreds of years, people have gone to war and killed one another for no other reason than that their religious beliefs differ. This continues to the present day. I have yet to hear of two scientists who have attempted to kill one another because their theories were at odds.

The church still has quite a bit of influence, but this explains why we haven't really studied consciousness as a sixth sense and how it became labeled as something evil. Also, because energy-based consciousness as a result of its repression for hundreds of years is not rooted in science, it doesn't get the scientific research it deserves. What scientist wants to be the one to blow the roof off religion? So many people practice one form of religion or another that it would be quite a challenge even now to get enough scientists to be willing to conduct studies that might draw us slightly away from religious beliefs. I believe, however, that you can have both religion and science and that they can coexist in harmony—for the most part, that is.

Chapter 28:

The Separation of Church and Science

It is so important to separate religion from this type of science, particularly because they overlap in so many ways. We have had religion for thousands of years, but we have only had science for hundreds of years. Many people are extremely passionate about their religion, some because they truly find happiness there and others because they were told they had to like it by their parents. Whatever the reason, those people will reject science if you don't differentiate the two. Religious folks reject the science of studying consciousness, and scientific people reject studying consciousness as a religion. That leaves a very small number of the population who accept and want to explore the science. Whatever your beliefs are, for any science to be taken seriously by the masses, it is important, I feel, to stay far away from religion. We start this by not stealing their "coined" terms and phrases.

So, I try not to use words like "spirituality" or a person's "soul." By my definition, the soul is one's own consciousness and/or awareness, and spirituality refers to a greater cosmic collective consciousness or a universal consciousness. I respect the lines that have been drawn between science and the church, which is how the church wants it to be. I also believe that it is better for science to keep its own terminology and differentiate itself. Let religion have the terms spiritual and soul. I will call it consciousness or energy.

When we die, our consciousness leaves our body and the energy within is stored in the dark energy in the universe all around us that we cannot see easily. You will catch a glimpse from time to time, however. Have you ever seen a shooting black line out of the corner of your eye, but when you look right at it, it's gone? Sometimes you "feel" someone is looking at you, and you notice a black line shoot across the room. That is dark ener-gy. Whether you believe that is the remains of someone's humanity in the form of energy created from their mind's consciousness, well, that is up to you, but I am relatively certain of it, especially since I have a few rather interesting thoughts when these "lines" present themselves. Seeing the line followed by vibrations inside my body or the other way around tells me there is someone or something that wants to communicate with me.

The dead in the fourth realm or dimension usually try to reach out to me; rarely is it the other way around. They have no concept of time, or they simply don't care. I'm not sure which. It doesn't really matter because I can choose to connect with them or not. It's up to me now. It's on my terms.

When I try to make contact, I usually look to my guides and masters. I believe their realm is higher, and it will take a little longer for me to get on that frequency, so to speak. Remember, they can tell me to go take a hike as easily as I can tell the ones in the fourth realm to do the same.

It would seem, however, that the more I am willing to help those who request my assistance, the more help I get in return from those I seek to communicate with. Yes, folks, there seems to be Karma after death too. Probably more so, in fact.

"I Feel You" (Journal Entry—Summer, 2019)

It was nighttime, so I climbed into bed and meditated for a little while. I then looked for something to watch on television. As I did this, I began to have the feeling that someone or something was making an attempt to connect with me. I could feel high vibrations, high up in my body from my shoulders up, which would typically mean the message was positive.

My immediate reaction to this was, "Not now, go away." However, I had been doing this a lot lately. It seemed that I always connected with the low vibrations, which meant a serious message of importance, and I kicked the high vibrations or good messages away from me. Therefore, I decided to allow the connection. It was still rather strong. I apologized for saying "not now" and "go away." I invited the energy to connect with me, and I asked them to raise their frequency. I did the same to connect quickly, but it never happened. The energy remained in the room, but it didn't connect.

My interpretation is that it is not easy for these energies to connect with me any more than it is for me to connect with them. It makes sense to me that they are fighting to come through. However, beings at higher levels or realms of existence, who perhaps are more evolved energies, such as guides or masters, can get through with ease if they choose to. These beings have enormous power, and you would not want to reject their messages, as they could be very important. Usually, they come alone or in groups of three or seven. The more often I connect with them to exercise my abilities, the more I will be able to help those outside my realm come through more easily. It seems to be just like anything else: the more you practice, the better you will get at it.

CHAPTER 29:

Energy Healing and Medicine—Let's Not Get Too Crazy

Energy healing refers to the healing of the energy that flows through you and your chakras. Having this done multiple times myself, by a certified master Reiki practitioner, has proven to be one of the most important things I have ever done. It was my first spiritual clearing followed by my first energy healing that enabled me to connect to the afterlife so easily. I told this story earlier in the book of how the floodgates just seemed to open up after I had those experiences with her.

That being said however, in the United States of America, we have absolutely the best medicine, the best doctors, the best medical researchers, and the best drugs in the world. Science-based medicine for the cure of illnesses should always be sought and should not be replaced by an energy healer alone.

Energy healing is awesome and feels great, as it can open you up to an entire new world by removing blockages in your energy flow that can build over time.

I am not what I would call an energy healer at this point in my life, but there is one thing I have done, and it is pretty cool, if I do say so myself.

I called upon my guides and the conscious universe while putting myself in a deep meditative state. Someone up there must be willing to help me with this. I can call upon one of those folks who want me to get a message to their widow, widower, or some other loved one in the land of the living and say, "Hey, dead person, you help me, and I will help you. What do you say?"

Just make sure you hold up your end of the bargain if you go this route.

They can pass these amazing super high euphoric vibrations that feel better than sex. I have no words to describe it, but we all know how good sex feels.

This is no easy task for me, mind you. I have to use all of my natural energy to do it, but I can pass the vibrations through me to the other person by touching them. I have done this with Jessica when she's had a really bad day. It is best if your loved one is in a meditative state to receive this, and I never tell them I am going to do it just in case I can't perform for some reason, but I have never had that problem yet.

I summoned upon any and all beings out there listening and asked them to help Jessica with every fiber of my being. I could feel it a little bit, but it passed through me quickly. The benefit went to Jessica. Afterward, I was completely spent and could barely stay awake. When Jessica opened her eyes, she described what she felt as the most amazing euphoric "dream", which made it all worthwhile. This is the journal entry of that experience.

"Feel This?" (Journal Entry—Summer, 2019)

Jessica said one night when we got together, "I do not want to go out. Let's stay home and order food and stay outside in the gazebo." "Let's meditate."

I agreed.

I decided to see if I was actually able to pass positive feelings from the universe through me to her. This was on a whim and completely experimental on my part. I placed my hand on her back close to her neck and focused all of my energy on her happiness. I asked the universe to give her this. I asked her father to give her this. I asked anyone listening to give her this. What happened next was extraordinary. She told me after coming out of her meditation that she had felt something wonderful, and that she had never experienced anything like it during a meditation session before. She saw dazzling, swirling colors of light and awoke giggling, happy, relaxed, and positive.

My interpretation is that I can pass feelings and thoughts through me to her and maybe to others. I am happy about this ability to see the transformation of someone I love. It is not, however, particularly pleasant for me physically. It isn't terrible, but it's not pleasant either. My head gets hot and red. I also lose energy and become tired, and sometimes, I get a headache.

"Don't Cry for Me" (Journal Entry—Winter, Early 2020)

The date was March 8, 2020. This story began about two months before this date, in the first few weeks of the new year. It involved an old friend. I don't mean he was old. I mean that we had been friends for over 20 years. He was very near and dear to me and had been there for me countless times through difficulties in my life. We had regrettably lost contact a few years prior to this. We always sent each other a happy birthday or a quick hello or Merry Christmas, but we were no longer a part of one another's lives. Nonetheless, no matter how much time had passed, I knew I could pick up the phone and rely on him for anything and vice versa.

He began to come into my mind more and more frequently at the turn of the new year, but I did not know why. At this point, I was not getting that anything detrimental was happening involving him, but admittedly, I did not stop to meditate on it or try to get more information either. I was so consumed with my own life and activities that I didn't see the signs.

In the last week of February, I received a phone call at work from a mutual friend of both of ours, who said my friend was in the hospital, but he didn't know why and could I please find out what was going on. "Of course I will," I assured him. I came to find out my friend had a staph infection, something you can get from being in any medical facility. He had been thinking of having a hip replacement and had to have an assortment of tests run to make sure he was physically fit for surgery. A matter of weeks later, he admitted himself to the hospital for complications of a staph infection. He was given a full spectrum IV of antibiotics, which should have cleared it up. Millions of people get staph infections each year.

He and his family all expected that he would be treated and sent home. Everyone but me. I was the only person in the world that knew he wasn't going home. When I finally looked into and meditated with my friend's situation in mind, I saw it. I saw his death. I begged and pleaded to anyone listening to please not let this be true. "Please, let me be wrong! I beg of you, just this once, allow me to be wrong! He has kids. He is only in his 50s. He must live. They need him!"

These are the times I don't want this ability. People tell me I have a gift. What fucking kind of gift is this? This is complete torture. Who the fuck would call this a gift in their right mind? How could I go visit him in the hospital now knowing his destiny? What would I say to him? I am sure he would have loved to know life doesn't just end here and everything goes black, but I couldn't tell him that. I'm sure he thought he was going home one day at that point.

The disease worsened, as I already knew it would. I was in contact with his sister, who was there daily. She was so optimistic. It was killing me inside. When I went to visit, I told him he was a fighter and that he would get through this. But all I really wanted to do was tell him the truth. I wanted to tell him that it's not bad at all to die. I wanted to tell him to get his affairs in order, say goodbye, and get ready for a really cool adventure into the light. I couldn't say any of that! I'd never lied to this man in my life. I thought he would see right through me, but I continued to be optimistic and tell him I was sure he would be better soon.

A few days later, I got the phone call that I already knew was coming. He'd died. It didn't make the call any easier to get. It still hits me as I sit in my office chair and stare at the wall. Sadness begins to take me over. I know I need to break down and cry to process this, but I rarely allow myself to cry. I always thought it wasn't a manly thing to do, I suppose. What happened next will show you the type of completely selfless, good-hearted, caring person he was.

While staring at that wall I entered an altered state and he came to me in a vision, and he refused to let me cry. He said, "You will not cry for me."

Each time I began to break down, I would feel these very high, tingly vibrations inside my body. They were almost euphoric in nature, and each time I tried to cry, I found myself wanting to laugh a little instead.

"You will not cry for me," he said again.

He appeared three times in a twenty-four-hour period after his death. Each time I tried to cry, he would come back and not allow me to do so. Each time, he filled my body with these high vibrations that felt like they were tickling my brain. He wasn't angry at me for not telling him, and just like in life, he worried about me more than himself even after his death.

CHAPTER 30:

Actions Speak Louder Than Thoughts

This is something I must constantly continue to remind myself. Since I am able to be in a room or in a conversation with someone and pick up a thought or two that they are experiencing, I should never react to it before it is said or done. This has deeply affected my personal relationships. Just because someone is thinking about something doesn't mean they will act on it or do it, and there is no point in arguing over a thought that may never become an action. Imagine my children having a mischievous thought and dad says, "Don't even think about doing that." Now apply that to everyday life.

This can really destroy a relationship, especially with your spouse. Just because she had a thought to herself that she would love to go on a shopping spree when you both agreed to be saving for a new house, or that the guy over there is good looking, it doesn't mean anything, and I have to remember to throw it away and not react to what is just a thought. I have had a difficult time with this admittedly. I can anticipate and react when nothing would have happened anyway.

Now imagine I am at work and one of my employees, as I am speaking to them, thinks to themselves, "This guy [meaning me] is a frigging jerk." This thought floats into their minds at the same time I am really trying to help them overcome a problem with their work. What would you do? Could you throw it away? You would have to, trust me, or you will have a miserable existence. People think stuff. It's not a big deal. Some stuff will be good and some things will be bad, but remember, unless the words are followed up by an action, you must remember to throw them away. It's a meaningless thought that they may not even agree with normally.

Think of it this way. A car cuts you off, and you are so angry, you call this driver every name in the book, and then you realize the driver is your cousin who you love dearly and that they just made a mistake in the moment. The same happens with thoughts. One minute we think we hate someone we just met at a party and an hour later, after getting to know them, we think the person is actually kind of cool. If you only read the one thought, you would dislike this person unjustly. Remember to throw it away.

If you feel a loved one is having negative thoughts about you, a better approach to this is to ask them a question such as, "Is there something on your mind you want to talk about?" This gives the other person a chance to decide if they really want to talk about the thought or not. You can then find out if it is just a random, passing, in-the-moment thought or something they actually wish to address.

Your loved ones may not be thrilled with the fact that you know some of their thoughts. Put the shoe on the other foot. Imagine they know what you are thinking. If you have this ability, remember to tread lightly. It is a double-edged sword for sure.

The following exchange is an example of a conversation with Jessica where I reacted to thoughts before Jessica answered the questions.

Ray: Hey, babe, I found several literary agents who may be interested in representing me.

Jessica: Great!

Ray: There is one whose office is near your home. Do you know of Mr. John Doe?

Jessica: Um…

Ray: No?

Jessica: Well…

Ray: Well, I thought I would ask.

Jessica: …

Ray: Who do you think I should bring this book to first, babe?

Jessica: I think…

Ray: No. I knew you were thinking about her.

Jessica: What?

Ray: I would rather not bring it to her just yet because…

Jessica: Ummm… Excuse me, Ray, but are you having a conversation with yourself? Are you just going to keep answering for me before I actually say anything? Do I get to answer my questions verbally or will you just continue to telepathically extract the answers from my head?

We both laughed hysterically. This doesn't happen all the time, but she and I are so connected, sometimes it is like we have one brain.

"Pass That Back" (Journal Entry—Summer, 2019)

Jessica and I were in bed, discussing our differing interpretations of one of her father's messages, and all that had been happening. After some time, we just lay there and Jessica said "Feel my heart racing." I touched her and, clearly with significant presence there in the room, she began to feel euphoric. I was passing energy through to her that would change her emotional state for the better.

"This is the most amazing feeling," she said.

"I wish I could feel it too."

She proceeded to push me on my back and place her hand on my heart, and as she did, she transferred the feeling of euphoria. However, the feeling left her body, so I then touched her and said, "I want you to have it." We spent the next hour transferring this euphoria through touch and concentration to one another. We had complete control of the euphoric feelings and were able to pass them back and forth. The feeling was so strong, we each began to laugh when we were given the feelings. These are the moments that make this journey the most pleasurable and unforgettable.

My interpretation is that Jessica's dad was there and letting us know this was going to work out and be fine. He also was showing us that we needed each other.

CHAPTER 31:

The Language of Light

"Practice Makes Perfect" (Journal Entry—Winter, 2019)

One night while lying in bed, I decided to meditate before watching TV and after doing some reading. I find it easier to meditate after having read for a while, as I am able to go deeper into a state of trance more quickly. Attempting to connect to my guides, I began the exercises that my teacher had taught me to do.

Request a number from your guides. Get the number. Thank your guides for the number and repeat it back to them. Do this several times to open the connection with them more easily. This day, however, I could not get any numbers at all, which was unusual.

Then I tried for animal shapes. I got two random animals followed by Jessica's cat, Jessica's dog, and then the back of Jessica's head. That's strange, I thought.

I said, "What is this? Why are you giving me this?" The reply I got was like no other reply I had ever received. What I saw in my mind's eye were large black letters scrolling across an off-white screen. I read it three times as it scrolled across the screen to be sure of what I was seeing.

It said, "Take care of Jessica."

I paused and asked, "How do I know you are one of my guides or masters?" I got nothing back. I said, "How do I know you are not John [Jessica's father]?" As I said that, I received a sound in both of my ears that was almost deafening. A high-pitched hideous sound combined with a loud ringing in both of my ears at the same time. It rattled and vibrated my entire head very uncomfortably. It really shook me up because I had never heard or felt anything like this before.

I put both hands over my ears, but that did not affect the level of the volume because the sound was only in my head—it wasn't something anyone else could hear. The loud uncomfortable noise lasted about two seconds. It was extremely powerful and came in through the top of my head, vibrated down to my shoulders and back up again, and out through the top of my head. I immediately opened my eyes and looked around. Everything was gone. The sound, the vibrations, and the feeling.

I originally thought it was Jessica's dad, but after speaking with my teacher about this particular experience, she explained that what I heard was "light language," which can usually come from a being such as a guide or master. She explained, "Eventually you may be able to interpret the language. Just give it time." I wasn't sure I wanted to hear this noise again. It was like they were very angry with me.

"Can you Hear Me Now?" (Journal Entry—Winter, Late 2019)

It was the night of November 11, 2019. I was meditating without any purpose, just trying to connect for no particular reason. Quite quickly, I began to "hear" the sound of this light language in my mind's ear. This was a higher pitch than I had heard on previous occasions. At first, it sounded distant and faint. I asked my guide to kindly translate what it meant for me, and it then became much louder in my head. The sound wasn't annoying, and it didn't rattle and vibrate my whole head like the last time. It wasn't what I would call pleasant, but it wasn't necessarily unpleasant either. I was no longer frightened by it, so I continued to ask for clarification and an interpretation, but to no avail. Eventually, the sound became faint and eventually disappeared.

My interpretation is that this is a new form of communication (at least to me) that I have been receiving, but until I can decode it or understand its meaning, I won't be able to understand these messages. Also, I have noticed that my overall communication with my guides is much more relaxing for me now. Perhaps I am less frightened by it, as it seems to be flowing more freely and calmly. At the time of writing, I feel like I am evolving, becoming more astute with my abilities and allowing messages to flow much more freely into me.

"Hear and There" (Journal Entry—Winter, Late 2019)

It was November 20, 2019, and Jessica and I were in bed. I was very tired, but I couldn't fall asleep. I began to meditate. Immediately, I began to hear the sound of what I was told to be light language. I hear it often now. The volume often fluctuates, as does the pitch, but I am unable to identify what the differences mean. I also cannot interpret the actual meaning of the language, but that doesn't seem to matter or prevent me from getting other messages while hearing it.

I am now able to connect to the other side and be completely cognizant of what is happening around me. I can speak to Jessica and communicate with another realm at the same time. I can maintain both conversations, for lack of a better word. I've watched Medium Bonnie do this often. I'm making progress.

On this particular occasion, I saw something very disturbing. In this premonition, I was at a wake. The person who had passed was someone very close to me and is also very much alive at the time of writing this. Everyone at the wake was completely devastated. What do you do when you know you are going to lose someone before they know?

I told Jessica while I was still connected what I was seeing, and I began to get very emotional. I rarely get emotional like this. I have been to many funerals, and I accept that death is a part of life, but I love this person very much. I had known of some health issues, but nothing that should cause death at this point in time. I wasn't aware of anything terminal in nature. I felt like there was something I was supposed to say or do before it's too late. I wanted to say that everything is alright, that the other side is absolutely beautiful, and there is nothing to fear, but of course I can't do this. I can't distinguish when this will happen. There is nothing I can see in this premonition alerting me to the date, month, or year, for that matter. No one knows any of this may be coming. I do not want it to be true. This is really fucking up my head. Please don't let this one be accurate. Just let me be wrong.

Update: The health of this person took a significant turn for the worse just before publishing. For privacy reasons all I can say is significant. Fuck!

"Can you turn it down?" (Journal Entry—Winter, Late 2019)

I now can hear these sounds of light language regularly but at random times during the day and night. There are four different frequencies that I have noticed, two that I get only on the right side of my head, and two that are specific to the left side of my head. This allows me to know they are different energy beings on each side with different messages based on frequency or pitch. I'm getting closer to making sense of this, I think.

"Can you turn it down?" Update (Journal Entry—Spring 2020)

This took a while to figure out, admittedly, but the sounds are coming from my guides and masters. The right side is a particular guide that I know quite well, the one who told me to write this book in fact. He and I have become quite close. I can ask him yes or no questions and get answers by the frequency or pitch of the sound when he is around. He has never let me down.

This is how I figured this out. While in a slightly altered state during the day doing something mundane, I heard the sound on my right side. I decided to ask a series of yes or no questions. Some I knew the answers to. That's how I learned what meant yes and what meant no. This is exactly how they perform a lie detector test. They establish a baseline by asking you a series of questions that they know the answers to before they hit you with the test questions to see if you are being truthful. This is where I got the idea from. After many attempts and many different questions, I learned that the higher frequency or milder pitch meant yes (or the affirmative) and the lower louder frequency or pitch meant no (or the negative). He will also let me know if what I am doing, saying, or planning to do is a good or bad idea. So, for example, if I am talking with someone and I am saying something incorrect or something I shouldn't say at all, he will zap me with the no sound. This comes in handy, and I am very grateful for him. I just need to learn how to keep my big mouth shut long enough, for him to give me the go-ahead to say the next thing.

The left side is a completely different guide, and he is less communicative. His sounds are usually of serious warnings. When I hear from him, I usually have to stop what I am doing and try to go into a trance state to see what it is I need to know. In the past, it has often been something serious in nature. He has alerted me to stay away from certain people, or events, for example. I am very grateful for him as well.

Jessica and I were staying at a beach house for a few days in the late springtime. We were sitting in the backyard which overlooks the bay enjoying the sun and doing some yoga together. We noticed loud music coming from the house to our left. The folks renting that house appeared to be in their twenties and they were having a party of about fifty people or so. They were inside and outside their house and being somewhat loud as any party would normally be. It didn't bother us because the houses were aligned in such a way that there was a sizeable patch of land between us and them.

As I looked over at this party in full swing, both of my ears began to light up with loud ringing and different pitches in each ear at different volumes. The only commonality is that they were both the sound of a warning. I continued to stare at the house watching the guests come and go. Jessica said every time she had previously stayed in this area it was usually very quiet. She asked me what was wrong. I told her I am getting a severe warning to stay away from that house. "Why?" she asked. "Something terrible is going to happen in there."

I couldn't bring myself to tell her what it was. It was too horrific to share and I had no way of finding out if I was correct. If I was, what could I possibly do to prevent it? I was tormented inside. The warnings wouldn't stop and I kept seeing a crime take place over and over again in my mind.

Jessica persisted and continued to ask me what was wrong. I told her I was trying to think of a way to get everyone out of that house. At this point Jessica was adamant I tell her what I saw. I told her that she really doesn't want to know because then both of us would be tormented. "Let me save you from the torture of knowing, and just stay the fuck away from that house" I said.

I began to meditate asking for answers. "What can I do?" I asked repeatedly. Jessica could tell I was emotionally and even physically affected by what I saw. She asked me once again to tell her and just then, the warning sound went away. It was replaced moments later by police sirens. They were going to the party house! One police car was followed up by several more minutes later. Since the police were there, I explained to Jessica that I had seen a disgusting vision a sex crime involving a heavily intoxicated female. I don't know if the police had come before or after that incident. I can only hope it was before.

CHAPTER 32:

Light and Death

"The Worst Thing I've Seen" (Journal Entry—Winter, Late 2019)

I had not slept well for several nights. The continuing attempts of other energy beings trying to make contact with me in the evenings was becoming a problem. I had not yet mastered the art of shunning them away if I needed to. I had chosen to acknowledge and "answer" them this time due to their extreme persistence.

When I finally agreed to accept the request from the energy present in the room and went into a trance, I began to see a house. I could only view an extreme close-up of the exterior, the siding, or shingles of the house and the roof. The siding was mostly white but a bit dirty and scratched, and the roof was made with black shingles with a white pattern. The fact that it was very close up to my face made me think it might not be a pleasant thing I was about to see. When I see bad shit, it is very close to me. Almost as if I am sitting inches away from the movie screen.

I "stepped back," so to speak, to get a better view and entered a curved archway entrance that brought me into a room where I saw a man (most likely in his forties) on the left, standing up looking over and staring down at a much younger female (possibly in her teens) who was face down and not moving at all. I could make out the man's face a little bit, but I could only see the bottom of the girl's sneakers and back of her legs. Her sneakers had a distinct rubber pattern on the soles, like small x's inside of squares. I tried to stay and get more information, but I couldn't get anything else, and besides, this was so disgusting I had to leave. I just knew something terrible had happened and that he had done something to her.

I know that Medium Bonnie has used her abilities to help many law enforcement agencies solve crimes, but at this point, I don't know if I am witnessing a crime that is in the past, present, or future. I needed to get her advice.

"The Worst Thing I've Seen" Update (Journal Entry—Winter, Late 2019)

Approximately a day or so after the premonition, I received an email from a service provider to which I subscribe that sends out Megan's Law reports if a registered sex offender moves into your neighborhood. When I opened the email and clicked the link, there he was, the guy in the premonition above. He was a fucking sex offender and moved within a three-mile radius of my home after being released from prison. I assumed he had already been caught for the crime he committed, and I was receiving a warning.

"Help Me" (Journal Entry—Winter, Late 2019)

I received a very disturbing premonition while lying in bed. I saw a woman's face, and it had a blue shade to it with blue veins sort of popping out of her skin. It looked to me like no blood was getting to her head. She seemed like she had been strangled, drowned, or choked. She was reaching out to me with her right hand. She was on the floor in an attempt to crawl forward closer to me. That's when I realized she was asking for my help. She was dead and may have been murdered. This was the first time I had seen something of this nature and I didn't know what to do. I immediately backed off, so to speak. I then asked her what can I do? The next thing I saw jumped out in front of me. It was a monkey's face. The monkey was up super close to my face. I jumped back with fear.

Why was she showing me a monkey and why did she want me to be afraid of it? The dead often communicate with pictures because it is easier for them to relay than words. This was something I would learn later on in my teachings. None of this had any meaning to me personally, whatsoever. I was, however, very concerned for this woman. Was she murdered and wanted me to help find her killer? Was the monkey face a clue? What kind of message is this?

I was very shaken up because this was the first time I had seen an injured person or a dead person showing me the manner in which they died. The only thing I knew for certain was that she needed my help and I felt helpless. I asked her repeatedly to tell me what to do. "Please tell me what to do." I received nothing else and eventually she faded away.

Later in the same premonition after the woman left, I saw the outline of what might have been a face in the center of a circle and what appeared to be a light shining from around the back of the circle. The best way I can explain this, is that it was similar to an eclipse, but instead of the moon in front of the sun, it was someone's head. The light behind the head shone toward me. Behind the light that was emitting from the circle was complete darkness. It was almost as if the light was being emitted from this person's head. I cannot see a face, only a shadow. The light is too bright. It is warm and inviting.

No one other than him has appeared to me this way. No being has ever not had any light behind them. Then came a very peaceful feeling that took over my entire body. This removed the fear and the trembling I had from the previous vision. I did not know who he was at this point, but he has shown up before at some really difficult times during my premonitions. When he comes, everything negative disappears, a peaceful calm takes over, and I know what I am supposed to do next. Just his presence changes everything about me. A euphoric feeling accompanies him and goes directly into me. I see everything clearly. I am relaxed. I am no longer afraid. I feel great, and I know what to do. It is amazing.

There is no light behind him because I think he is the carrier of the light. I am calm and at peace, feeling euphoric vibrations through my body. It is the most incredible feeling, and I know I am in the presence of the Divine. I am grateful and honored to be there. He was there to tell me that he would help with what I had just seen and therefore, I didn't have to.

"Let Yourself Die" (Journal Entry—Winter, Early 2020)

On January 25, 2020, I arranged a meeting with my teacher Medium Bonnie. She was extremely busy with other projects, so she hadn't come to our area in quite some time. I was very excited that she was going to be in my area, and I took the opportunity to have face-to-face time with her.

We met at a local meditation center. We discussed the visions in which I saw what I thought might have been murders. She explained that the murdered woman, and most other energy beings that come to me, need help. A variety of different types of help. This one in particular might have been wanting me to help solve her murder. She reminded me that I have the ability to accept this type of communication and help the deceased. She told me I am a healer for the dead, in some cases a sort of therapist, if you will.

Energy beings immediately after their death can get stuck in the next realm immediately following their death, and need help to move on. They may need closure themselves. They may have something unfinished here on Earth and have difficulty moving on to a higher plane. This may be why they seek the help of mediums, people who can "see" them. I asked her why this woman showed me a monkey. She said it was the woman's way of communicating with me to the best of her ability. She would have continued to show pictures or other images that would help me solve the puzzle—the puzzle being her message.

Medium Bonnie asked me, "What do you think of, or about, when you see a monkey, like the one she showed you?" This is what you must ask yourself each time anyone like her gives you a picture of something, in order to figure out what they are trying to tell you. It is common for the dead to communicate this way. Since they can't talk easily to me, I must try to decipher the message through the pictures and/or metaphorical figures they show me.

Some energy beings can communicate with humans better than others. Some have the ability to come through easier than others. Medium Bonnie reminded me that they generally may have a challenging time coming through to us in our realm of existence. This is something they must learn to do and practice to get better at. Similarly, we must teach ourselves how to connect with them.

She suggested I announce to the universe that I will be available to help any energy beings who wish to "talk" to me at a certain time and place. Then, I should create a copper circle around myself, sit inside, and wait for them to come. This will help me practice and help them at the same time.

Then, she asked me to tell her more about the end of the premonition when I saw the being with no light behind him, which I did. I told her about how wonderful the feeling was, that this was not the first time he and I had met, and how every time was incredible.

I said, "He never speaks."

"No, Jesus never speaks."

"Jesus?" I asked.

She said again, "Jesus never speaks."

"He enters, he leaves, and all is fine in my world again."

"He is with you often," she said.

"You really think it is him?"

"What do you think?"

There was a long pause in our conversation before either of us moved on. Honestly, I didn't want to speculate too much on who this Divine energy may be. It really didn't matter to me that I identify exactly who it was, because whether it be Jesus, Moses, Mouhamed, The Buddha, or someone else, I was so honored, humbled and truly grateful just to have the experience. A more important speculation on my part would be, am I worthy of such?

175

We then discussed the release of this book and my apprehensions about doing so. I didn't tell her I was apprehensive, mind you, she just knew. She asked me if it was because I was still doubting my abilities and I said, "Yes, absolutely." She said I had to stop doubting myself. She told me that I was advancing in months what it takes most mediums years to develop.

She suggested that she and I go to a so-called haunted place or building and visit whoever may be there. We would do this together. She told me this is how she practiced and made herself much more confident years earlier when she was learning her craft. She traveled to the most "haunted" places she could find in the country to practice and hone her skills, and it helped her greatly. This idea scared the shit out of me, but I agreed to do it. She said she will set something up, and I will write about it afterwards and share everything with you.

There was a brief silence in the room, while she looked at me. I could tell she was receiving a message due to the pause in our conversation.

She returned to me and then said, **"You must let yourself die, Ray."**

"WHAT? What do you mean?" I responded, shocked and very confused.

"You won't publish the book because you know that once you do your life as you know it will no longer exist and you will become someone else. Just like in death, we transform into someone or something else. You must let yourself die," she said again, quite emphatically. "Do it now, or you may lose your opportunity. Just let yourself die."

I understood exactly what she was saying to me, but this was still scary as hell. What would happen if I released this information to the world? What would my new life be like?

Two days later, I began to draft a letter to send out to various agents and publishers. Holy shit. Am I about to die?

"The Fender Bender" (Journal Entry—Winter, Late 2019)

On November 19, 2019, my mobile phone alerted me that someone was at the front door of my house while I was at work. The camera and the motion detectors at my front door were activated. I looked and saw that it was my mother leaving the house to get into her car. I watched her get in, and I felt something was behind her car for some reason. I was focused on the rear of her car, but I didn't know why. The way the cameras on the house are situated, I couldn't view the back of her car. I decided to text her and ask her to please drive carefully. She texted back, "Okay." This was completely out of character for me to do, and I do not know what made me do it. Five or ten minutes later, she called to tell me that she had just been involved in a motor vehicle accident. Her car had been hit in the rear by another driver who was not paying attention to the road. The driver of the other car was an off-duty police officer. He was very apologetic towards my mom and got her help immediately. Neither of them had any significant injuries.

My interpretation is that I must learn to identify these feelings for what they are more accurately and more quickly if I am to use them to help anyone. This could have been much more serious in nature. I have got to stop doubting myself, but I continue to be my own worst skeptic. I continue to have apprehensions that inhibit me from acting on things, such as this, where prevention may have been effectuated. It's my own insecurities that are holding me back.

CHAPTER 33:

Super Powers?

Jessica always told me that I need more yoga in my life. I failed to see how it would necessarily help me evolve, but I think yoga is so attractive. I love to watch Jessica do yoga. There is just something about the movements, the grace, the skill, and the strength, not to mention the outfits she wears, which are basically tiny pieces of see-through clothing. Yes! Sign me up!

In all seriousness, however, I didn't yet see how this practice of bending and twisting myself into a tortuous "pretzel-like" position for an hour was supposed to help me spiritually. I simply couldn't see it. In addition to that, from a physical fitness perspective, I consider myself to be in excellent physical shape, and I pride myself on working out regularly. I push myself to my limits daily with my workouts. I doubted that yoga was going to push me to my limits like weight training did. So, the first time I took a class with Jessica, I figured I'd get a small workout in and I'd get to see Jessica in the skimpy outfits twisting herself around and sweating. I was good with that. I grabbed my open mind, a mat, and water bottle, and took a yoga class with Jessica and her yoga instructor, Stacey.

Here is what I learned that day, and mind you, this is strictly from my perspective. I know many yogis will likely disagree, but here are my own thoughts after this session with Jessica and her very highly skilled, well-advanced, yoga teacher.

Yoga is fucking hard! It is meant to be fucking hard! Well, at least Jessica's kind of yoga is, which, let me assure you, is not restorative or the gentle type in the least. It is meant to push you beyond your natural limits in harrowing positions for extended periods of time. It is meant to force you to overcome any mental or physical discomfort levels and break through them. Jessica and her teacher Stacey have given this type of yoga a name.

It's "Bad Ass Yoga." I feel it's similar to the Marine Corps basic training. "We will break you, and if we can't break you on this day, we will break you tomorrow. Namaste!"

Since then, I have taken a few different yoga classes of varying levels of difficulty, which were not as intense shall we say. But in yoga with Jessica and Stacey, unlike a drill Sergeant, they usually begin all nice and sweet, and they tell me that if it's too strenuous to go into a child's pose and relax there for a minute. Well, you see, the child's pose for relaxing is the equivalent of a Navy Seal team member ringing the bell during hell week to quit the military, with a tiny little bit of self-respect remaining. There is no fucking way I am going to ring the bell and concede to the fact that I am in over my yoga head.

You know what happens if you don't break? You feel accomplished and amazing. You feel like nothing can stop you. You also physically feel blood and energy flowing through parts of your body you didn't even know you had. This is not only physical in nature, but it is also mind over body. You begin with a mantra and dedicate the day's practice to something import-ant, but make no mistake, doing yoga with Jessica, and with Stacey as your instructor, it's going to be more like Ivan Drago in Rocky 4 for the next hour: "I must break you!"

That's Stacey and Jessica's "Bad Ass Yoga."

What is really happening here is you are mixing mental and psychological toughness with physical toughness and using the energy within yourself com-bined with the energy of others in the group collectively to achieve mental and physical goals that you did not know you could accomplish before.

Now that is fucking spiritual. Sign me up.

"The Message" (Journal Entry—Winter, Early 2020)

This particular week, Jessica had been telling me each and every day she had very strong feelings that I really needed to start practicing yoga as soon as possible. She didn't know why, or where this was coming from necessarily, but she knew it had to be. So, she booked us a private lesson for the weekend. I had done a couple of yoga moves previously with Jessica and a little at the retreat last summer, but never an actual class with a yoga instructor (this is prior to me being tortured by Jessica and Stacey in the last paragraph above). Jessica took the lesson with me, even though she was an accomplished yogi who was finishing her yoga teacher training at this time. She worked with the instructor to help teach something completely foreign to me.

We left the house, and it was a cold but clear day, without any precipitation in the forecast. We drove to the yoga studio and completed our yoga session, which was great. When we came out, there was an unexpected dusting of snow. I'd say there was just about a half inch of snow that lay on the ground beneath us. We both commented on how odd it was given the opposing weather forecast, but didn't think any more about it. On the drive home, Jessica and I discussed the class and the importance of yoga and meditation in our lives.

I thought that I definitely wanted to continue to learn yoga and challenge myself, as I had really enjoyed and respected the practice.

Driving down the street in Jessica's SUV, we pulled up to her house and made a left turn into her driveway. As we pulled in, I looked at the fresh snow that had just fallen on the ground while we were gone and calmly said, "Look, Jessica, it's a message." At about the same time, Jessica, noticed the same thing and shouted out, "Who the hell was in my driveway, and what is that?"

I said again, "It's a message." I don't know why I said that, I just knew it was some sort of message. Jessica didn't understand what I was talking about when I said it was a message, and she continued to drive up and over the message to the back of the driveway closest to the house.

I said, "You just drove over our message, babe."

"What do you mean by a message?" she asked. She proceeded to repeat her question of who was in the driveway? We walked over to the "message," which looked like a symbol of some type, imprinted in the fresh snow in the driveway. It was perfectly symmetrical and beautiful, with the exception of Jessica's tire tracks across it. It was about twelve feet long and six feet high. It was amazing, whatever it was, I thought. We just stared at it, not saying a word.

"I'm going to check the cameras," Jessica exclaimed, and she ran inside the house, while I remained outside.

In a tizzy, Jessica ran into the house and back out of the house. She stared at the symbol once again, ran back into the house, and then ran back out of the house again. "There's nothing on the cameras, nothing at all," she said. "No one was here. It just appeared." She was kind of freaking out a bit. "Someone, or something, somehow, someway, this symbol showed up on our property. What the fuck?" Jessica rarely curses. This was getting serious, I thought.

We both continued staring at it before Jessica said, "Oh my God. It's a fucking Lotus Flower."

I was silent and calm, counting the F-bombs.

"Ray, it's a fucking Lotus flower!" Oh my God! Oh my God! This is incredible; this is unbelievable! I have to get my camera, oh my God, oh my God, oh my God!

She was, all at once, laughing, crying, and running in and out of the house like a crazy person as I just stood there taking it all in.

So, I calmly said, "Um, what's a Lotus flower again?" I truly had no idea what she was referring to.

"You are! This is for you! This is for you, Ray! It is the symbol of yoga, and it is for you! Don't you see?"

"What?" I said.

I had no idea what a lotus flower was or how I could symbolically be one, but Jessica was beside herself with happiness, wonderment, and joy, so I went with it. We continued to take pictures of this perfectly symmetrical, five-petal Lotus flower that was given to us in the fresh snow, right after my first yoga class. Certainly, it was an amazing experience. When we went inside, she pulled up the flower and its meaning on the computer. When I read about the Lotus flower, it became that much more amazing.

Here is what we found relating to the symbolic meaning of the Lotus flower:

"The Lotus flower is regarded in many different cultures, especially in eastern religions, as a symbol of purity, enlightenment, self-regeneration, and rebirth. Its characteristics are a perfect analogy for the human condition: even when its roots are in the dirtiest of waters, the Lotus produces the most beautiful flower." (www.binghamton.edu)

"Wow! Okay, now I get it," I said to Jessica.

The Lotus flower grows out of dark, dirty waters and emerges above the water into an amazing thing of beauty. I suppose my life could be referred to in a similar way. Like Jessica said to me, I am the Lotus flower. The more this phenomenon sank into our heads, the more amazed we became by this mysterious creation. To this day, Jessica counts this in her top three things of crazy shit we have experienced together, and believe me, that is saying something! We have quite a long list of crazy shit. She cannot talk about this, even with me, without getting goosebumps and teary eyed, with a look of full amazement on her face.

To this day, every so often Jessica will ask me again, "That really happened, right?"

"Yes, baby, that really happened," I answered her.

That entire week, Jessica had been going on and on telling me that I must start taking yoga and about how it would change everything. I think it goes without saying that there couldn't have been a better symbol to send to me at that point in my life, right after my first official yoga class. Maybe I was becoming the more beautiful side of the flower.

"Sleepless Night" (Journal Entry—Winter, Late 2019)

I was going to bed at about 10 PM. I knew I would have trouble sleeping because I was feeling a sense of uneasiness. I took an over-the-counter cold medicine to make me feel drowsy so I could fall asleep easier, and it worked early on, but I woke up at midnight. I didn't know why, but after I woke up, I had an intense feeling that something was wrong, and it had Jessica's name all over it. I just kept replaying a recent conversation she and I had had over and over in my head. It came with an intense feeling deep inside me. The vibrations were low and deep. They were in a low part of my body, which usually means it is serious in nature.

I tried to meditate to see if someone or something wanted to make contact with me so I could find out the full message, but it didn't work. I became increasingly frustrated as time went on. I couldn't sleep and I could not get a message. Why was this happening? I tried to meditate again and focus on the feeling.

I reached out to Jessica's dad, but I could not make contact. This went on all night. I took more medicine to fall asleep, but still could not rest. By this time, I had taken enough medicine to knock out a horse, but still nothing. I was awake with this feeling that wouldn't let me go.

I finally fell asleep at about 6 AM and continued to wake up every hour or so. Luckily, it was a Saturday, so I didn't have to go to work. I got out of bed at about 1 PM, and the feeling was still there. I now felt like I was on the verge of a panic attack. I went to the gym to release some frustration, which helped a little bit, but once I got home and showered, the feeling came back as strong as ever.

Jessica and I had plans to go out to dinner that evening. I called her and explained I could not go out feeling the way did and asked if we could stay in. She was disappointed because she had been home for the past few days working from home and taking care of the kids, and she wanted to get out. She had also already booked a babysitter and felt bad canceling at the last minute. I knew she was displeased, so I reluctantly told her to go out without me, as we knew some of our friends were going to be at the restaurant already. I knew she wouldn't be alone once she got there.

At that point, however, the feeling within me was heightened to the point that I was almost hyperventilating. I asked again if we could please just stay home, and I told Jessica I would pay the babysitter even though we would not be going out. However, Jessica really wanted to go meet her friends, so I let it be, and we decided she would go to meet her friends without me. Ordinarily, this wouldn't be an issue, but something was very wrong; I didn't know what it was and I did not want to have a big argument with Jessica about it.

About ten minutes later, Jessica texted me that the babysitter had been in a car accident and would not be able to babysit. It was not a major accident and no one was hurt, but the babysitter wasn't coming any longer. Jessica jokingly said, "Okay universe, I get it, I'll stay home!" Little did she know it was at this moment that the feeling inside me of panic and the feeling that someone was shaking my insides like a tree branch in a hurricane almost completely went away. At this point, I was able to identify that the feeling was a way of telling me to keep Jessica home that night, and this was truly a serious matter.

I still had an uneasy feeling about something, but it was not as bad as when I was on the verge of a panic attack.

The bottom line was that if Jessica had gone out that night, something terrible would have happened. There is no doubt in my mind that Jessica's dad often alerts me to something bad that he can see in his daughter's immediate future and goes through me to get the message across. The strange thing was that he didn't identify himself (he always identifies himself somehow to me), and earlier I had tried to make contact with him, which I am often able to do easily since we have had so many communications, but I couldn't.

So if it wasn't Jessica's dad, who was giving me the warning? Was it me? Am I now able to foresee things more clearly? Up until this point, messages that are about someone other than myself come from a third-party source. For my entire life, I have always been able to foresee my own immediate future, but if the message was about another person, then the message usually comes from another person, whether they be living, dead, a guide, or a master.

Also, if it was me, then why was I unable to put my finger on the exact problem? All I knew was that this was serious in nature and it involved Jessica, which was certainly not enough for me to help prevent something from happening. The last message I received from the masters was "Take care of Jessica."

I am not sure who or what intervened that night. However, our friend who did go to the restaurant that night informed us later that she saw what I will call a person of disinterest in Jessica's life sitting at the bar with someone who is a person of interest to Jessica. If we had been there, this could have and most likely would have resulted in one or both of us losing our tempers for sure. It was a very good thing we did not go there that night.

"The Seance" (Journal Entry—Winter, Early 2020)

January 28 is marked in my calendar and labeled as "Jessica's worst day" because it is the anniversary of her dad's death. This year, I wanted to see if I could somehow make it less of a bad day for her. I came up with the idea of trying to channel her dad and allowing them to speak directly to each other. Boy, haven't I come a long way from being petrified of this stuff!

Channeling is a very advanced type of mediumship, so I have never attempted to do this. I have little idea of what I'm doing, but I know I can reach and speak to her dad. I have done that many times, but this time I was attempting to channel someone, and that is on another level. Channeling would allow him to actually enter my body to speak directly to Jessica without me being much of a middle man.

I rented us a hotel room, so we could be undisturbed, and I told her to bring a personal item of his and about six of the battery-powered candles from our yoga room at Jessica's house. I would have used real candles, but they might have set off the smoke alarm in the hotel. The candles were used to make a circle that we could sit in. I understand a copper circle is the better way to go, but I didn't have any copper lying around. I wanted to leave one or two lights on because her dad is notorious for blinking electrical lights or televisions or whatever electrical is available to him.

We sat in the circle and began to meditate. Jessica had her dad's eyeglasses, a note handwritten by him, and a few pictures. I didn't really know if I needed those things, but it sounded like a good idea. It didn't take John long to appear on the movie screen in my mind. He is powerful and abrupt. Remember earlier in this book I told you about Medium Joe, a veteran medium who channeled him and was brought to tears by John's overwhelming presence inside of him?

As John got closer and closer to me, the vibrations intensified. He began to send messages, which I relayed. Some I understood, but others only made sense to Jessica, of course. This was fairly typical so far. As the vibrations worsened, I began to feel extremely nauseated. At one point, I had to stop and go get a garbage pail to place in front of me in case I threw up. Jessica told me she didn't mind if I wanted to stop, but I wasn't stopping now. No way. He was so close to entering me, I could feel him. He was right there in the upper right-hand quadrant of my mind's eye. That is his spot. That is where he always begins, but this time I wanted things to be different. Come down off the screen this time, John.

In a more traditional or typical visit, the different beings I interact with come out of different places in my mind's eye and appear on the movie screen. For example, one of my guides always begins in the lower right-hand corner if he is visiting me. My panel of three guides is always at my two o'clock on the screen in my mind's eye. Everyone seems to have their individual spot of entry on the screen, and it never changes. I was trying to get John off the screen to enter my physical being.

I asked John to come closer, and when he did, I began to get drastically sicker. My dinner was coming up for sure. I was in such a deep state of trance that I could not feel most of my physical body. From what I could tell, drool was coming down my cheek, my head was moving slightly up and down, and my body was swaying back and forth slowly. Everything began to tremble inside. It was as if there was a hurricane inside my body. Each minute, the feelings got stronger and stronger. John started to pull back. I asked him, "Where are you going?" He said, "I'm going to make you much too sick. You're not ready for this."

He was right. I was not ready for this. Not at this point in time. I think he was appreciative that I tried, and I know I made it a slightly better day for my love, Jessica.

CHAPTER 34:

Video on Demand

"Oh, I See" (Journal Entry—Fall/Winter, 2019)

Jessica and I had an argument. We had been emailing things back and forth and talking less by phone at night. (She and I did not live together.) When I dwelled on the argument, I began to "see" her in my mind. She was at her house, and I was in mine some 15 miles away. These scenes were a bit more colorful, and the events were closer to real time. At the time, I called it real-time clairvoyance, but I later learned it is called remote viewing.

I could see her in the kitchen.

I texted her and I asked what she was doing, she said, "Feeding the kids."

I thought, Okay, that is just one time. I got lucky.

The next one I saw her in the bathroom with the kids. Later we spoke and she said, "I just gave them their showers and I am getting them into bed."

Still, I could just have known the schedule. Day three, it was the third time and I saw them (her and the two kids) in her room in her master bed. The kids had a kids' show on TV and were arguing over something, and Jessica was on her phone maybe reading or texting someone. I texted her to say goodnight. She said goodnight and told me that she had to go because the kids were fighting. I mistakenly said, "I know." I don't think she caught it, however.

A few days later, we had talked everything out and I told her, "I think I have real-time clairvoyance and don't get freaked out, but I can sometimes see you."

"Um, what?" she said.

"I can see you."

"You can't do that!" she exclaimed.

"Well, yes I can actually, Jessica."

She jokingly replied, "Isn't there some type of psychic's code of conduct or ethics you guys must follow?"

"I think so. I'll look into it for you." I laughed.

"So I can report you then?" Jessica said jokingly.

I said, "I think we have a board of master psychics who make the rules. I'll send you their website to fill out the online complaint form." She began to laugh.

"Yes," she said. "Thank you. You're going to lose your psychic license."

"Stop. You're killing me. I can't stop laughing."

"Privacy violations are taken very seriously from what I understand."

A little while later, I couldn't help but think about her once again, and she texted me out of nowhere: "Stop looking at us! The lights are flickering on and off, and you are scaring the children."

I texted back, "I'm so sorry. I will find something to watch on television immediately."

I took my remote control and clicked on any show to watch to get mind on something else and off her. As soon as I began watching (which occupied my mind), she texted back, "Thank you. It has stopped now."

Remote viewing and flickering lights? What's next?

"Who's That Girl?" (Journal Entry—Winter, Early 2020)

On January 13, 2020, while lying in bed with Jessica at her place just before going to sleep, I began to get vibrations that were high and tingling and rather pleasant in nature. I knew there was a presence in the room, and so

I suggested we meditate. When we did, I got a vision of a woman who was smiling brightly with the sun on her face walking barefoot in the grass. I was able to see her from the chest up and from her knees down. No middle section, but this was the most of any person on the other side I had ever seen thus far. She had something in her left hand that she wanted to give to someone. I think it was for Jessica. I couldn't see the item because it was all black, but I "felt" it was some sort of family heirloom or piece of jewelry. Before coming out of the meditation, I asked Jessica if she knew who this was by describing the woman's facial features, the fact I knew there was a relationship to her dad, the woman's approximate age, and what was in her hand. The woman was wearing a blue and white kerchief on her head. Her clothing was very conservative. She wanted to let us know that she was very happy.

Jessica thought it might be her grandmother, so I asked for a picture of her. Jessica said that her grandmother would allow her to play with her jewelry as a child when visiting her house. In fact, as Jessica describes, it's one of the things she remembers most about her, the jewelry. She showed me a few pictures on her phone, and as I went through the old photos, Jessica went to let our dog out. When she got outside, on the ground was a blue and white kerchief. When Jessica returned to the bed, she told me what she'd found outside on the ground and then I showed her a picture of the woman I saw from her phone. It was in fact her grandmother on her dad's side.

Jessica's grandmother had battled with depression most of her adult life. Jessica said to me she couldn't really remember a particular time when her grandmother was really happy. She couldn't seem to find her happiness here on Earth, but her message on that day was very clear: "I am very happy here and now." Jessica began to cry with tears of joy that her grand-mother was at peace and in a good place. It took her a lifetime of anguish to have peace and happiness after death.

These events are becoming increasingly normal to me and significantly easier to identify and decode.

Chapter 35:

Becoming Limitless

You don't realize this yet, but you are already limitless. Nonetheless, I am going to show you how to harness the power you already possess to push yourself beyond what you think your limits are now. You can accomplish absolutely anything you wish. Here are the steps. Some I have already mentioned previously, but I'll reiterate them here because of their importance.

1. Take the absolute worst, negative shit from your life, roll it into a ball, place it into your core-being, and use it to fuel your fire. Utilize that which will propel you to the next level of success in your existence.

2. Remember this quote: "I have learned far more from my pain than I have ever learned from my pleasures." Each painful experience has taught me a life lesson that I would never have learned in any textbook. You have these as well. Although they differ, you can and must learn from them.

3. Find your "Why." What is the reason you want to accomplish your goals? You had better be willing to die for your why, or you are just wasting your time and energy.

4. "You are the sum of your peers." Get rid of your friends who have no ambition or drive. The ones who see everything negatively. You can be friendly, but limit your time with them or limit your conversations with them. They will subconsciously bring you down to their level. At best, you will only be slightly more successful than the best ones in your group. Therefore, get a better group.

5. Quit using recreational drugs and alcohol if you use them. Even in moderation, these will limit your abilities significantly. You won't realize it, but other people around you will.

6. Do at least one thing each day that benefits only yourself. For example, eat right, exercise, learn something, read a book, or take a class. Do one selfish thing to get yourself to feel good and get closer to your goals.

7. Do at least one thing each day that benefits only someone else. For example, teach, motivate, educate, or give. By helping others get closer to their goals, others will want to help you in return. This act of kindness will come back to you many times over. It's Karma, baby!

8. Meditate daily. If you do it regularly and get really good at it, it will open up doors and unlock your mind. Exercise your brain by meditating as often as possible. You'll eventually tap into the world's universal, collective consciousness. This takes time to do. Do not give up, however. This is how you will tap into your sixth sense, and if you already have it partially developed, then it will get you to the next level of your abilities. This rule may be the most important one up here, so don't ignore it.

9. Trust your gut instincts. As you develop your conscious being, your gut feelings will increase in accuracy over time. Keep a journal of these experiences. This will allow you to learn the difference in the feeling you get when you "just know something."

10. Exercise your physical body. A healthy body means a healthy mind. Try to work out, swim, bike, or do whatever you like. Just do it.

11. Spread the love. Literally. Tell your loved ones how you feel about them each time you speak with them. A simple "love you" is all it takes at the end of a conversation, email, text message, or anything. Remember, you really have no idea if it is the last time you will ever speak to them.

12. Be grateful for all you have and are. Don't say things like, "I have to go to work today" or "I have to take care of my kids." Instead, say, "I get to go to work today" and "I get to take care of my kids."

13. Trust the signs. Remember, there are no coincidences. You are probably getting messages right now and don't realize what they are.

14. Wake up each day and act as if this will be your last day on Earth, because one day you'll wake up and you'll be correct. Do not fear that day, but welcome it, for your journey has just begun.

The Formula

I spoke in an earlier chapter about a process in which one could change the perception of oneself within their true reality and that this process could manifest permanent positive changes in one's reality. I am going to share this method with you.

According to Buddha, there is such a process, but there is a catch. Here are Buddha's Five Precepts to Enlightenment. It was said by Buddha that you must live by these five to reach your full enlightenment. I still struggle with some of them. I am not Buddha, by any means, but I'm trying. (Damn those meatballs are delicious!)

1. Refrain from taking any life (i.e., killing any living creature).

2. Refrain from taking what is not freely given (i.e., theft).

3. Refrain from sexual misconduct (i.e., committing sexual offenses).

4. Refrain from harmful speech (i.e., lying, name calling, or gossiping).

5. Refrain from intoxicants that cloud the mind (i.e., drugs or alcohol).

As you know, I once struggled with the use of drugs and alcohol. However, through the various forms of meditation that I have learned, I can make myself feel better than any alcohol or drug could ever make me feel. I can make real change that is permanent in myself, my life, and my perceptions of both. I no longer feel like I am missing something in my life or that there is anything I cannot have if I really want it. I no longer wish to alter my perception of reality with the use of intoxicants because my real life is extraordinary. I don't have any reasons to want to escape it.

You really can have everything. You can live without wanting. You can be happy just "being." I promise you. Here is the formula:

1.   Meditate (get great at it)

2.   Practice Karma (be kind to others)

3.   Manifest (meditate your wants)

4.   Practice Mindfulness (live only in the present moment)

5.   Live by Buddha's Precepts (to the best of your ability)

Meditation is crucial to this process. Aligning yourself with the universal structure and consciousness is both physical and psychological in nature. It takes mental clarity and practice to accomplish. This is where we all have the ability to connect, be limitless, have limitless knowledge and potential, and acquire all the things we want.

In my opinion, it is by far the greatest experience one can ever have as a human.

This connection can take place through the practice of meditation as Buddha said and did; it is the ultimate enlightenment one can achieve. Removing any and all obstacles between you and the universal collective consciousness is what takes time and practice. The good news is that you do not have to reach full enlightenment to begin to manipulate your reality and get the things you want out of life.

Begin each day with a brief mediation. Think about all the things you are grateful for, followed by what you want in life. This can be as brief as five minutes if necessary. As you continue through your day, be kind to the people you interact with. Random acts of kindness will return to you many times over. If you have a difficult day, sneak away and repeat the brief morning meditation with the affirmation. It takes but a minute or two. Practice being mindful and live life only in each of its present moments. You have the choice of not allowing yesterday's negative decisions be repeated in your present moment. Live each day by Buddha's Five Precepts to the best of your ability and end your day with a meditation before bedtime. Make this one longer. Begin with an attitude of gratitude and state all of what you have to be thankful for. Things like your loved ones, your job, a kind word from someone, the opportunity to care for your children, and your health. Follow this again by what you want next out of life. Then just relax, clear your mind, and see where it takes you. Wake up and repeat.

Take the formula and then write your book. I can't wait to read it!

CHAPTER 36:

Divine Intervention

"The Next Chapter" (Journal Entry—Winter, Early 2020)

This book has always been a work in progress. Things that transpired were added as they happened for the most part in real time. My birthday is February 15, and this year (2020) was rather special. Here is why. Three days before the fifteenth Jessica took me away to celebrate my birthday. She and I enjoy doing a lot of meditating when we travel, and this time was no exception. When we meditate together, the effects are multiplied. It can be very powerful to meditate in a group or even with just one other person.

After one of our sessions, we began to reminisce about how we got here and the events that unfolded throughout our shared lives—most of which are in this book. Jessica came across a picture that was drawn for her by Medium Joe, the famous medium and artist. He draws the things he sees in the afterlife. I wish I could draw. I simply do not have that talent.

The picture is of her father. Medium Joe drew it the first time Jessica went to see him to make contact with her dad. Medium Joe was the first medium to make contact with her dad. Anyway, when she showed me this picture, I jumped up and exclaimed, "That's him! That's your dad!"

Jessica said, "I know."

I said, "I realize you know, but what you don't know is that is exactly the way I saw him in my vision. That is the same way he had his hair, beard, and mustache, and he was wearing that same shirt." This was the shirt I was trying to explain earlier in this book.

If you recall the story of my meeting with Jessica's dad, one of the things that stood out was that he did not resemble the photos I had previously seen of him, and he was wearing a distinctive shirt. So, you see, Medium Joe, who is a legendary medium, saw her dad exactly the same way I did, in every way. This was a huge validation for me. But the story doesn't end there.

Jessica decided to show me who Medium Joe was by going to his website. When we got there, it said, "Interviewing now for our two-year psychic medium educational program. Deadline to register is February 15, 2020." That was my birthday, and I had three days to register. Is this a coincidence? Had we not gone away, Jessica would not have pulled out the picture, so she would not have taken me to the website, and I would not have known that I had three days remaining to register and get interviewed by Medium Joe. Jessica asked me if I would register.

I replied with, "Are you kidding me? I have to." This was a universal intervention that I was not going to mess with.

I applied to Medium Joe's program. The first hurdle was to complete an interview sheet in its entirety and send it back to his assistant. The sheet contained essay questions that were quite personal in nature. I emailed back my reply and waited. I waited, and I waited, and I waited. Nothing came back. I started to think that maybe I am not really a psychic medium and that this is all in my head. Yes, I am back to chapter one in this book with self-doubt about my abilities again. But if I have this ability, then Medium Joe would surely know just like Medium Bonnie, my other teacher, knew before we had met.

I sent a follow-up email asking for my status, but I received nothing in response. Then came the phone call. I didn't recognize the phone number calling me, but I just knew I had to answer it. I had no idea why. I typically have my assistant answer my phone because more often than not, someone is trying to sell me something and she will screen them for me.

I answered and heard, "Hi, Raymond. This is Medium Joe, how are you?"

Holy shit, it's him! I was nervous, but I knew he wouldn't be calling me if I had no chance of being chosen. He went on to share some personal things with me that I will not talk about here, but I will tell you that he was able to understand my life and where I was coming from based on his vast experiences. He knew things that I had not yet revealed to him about myself. He just "knew" them already.

I sighed with huge relief after hanging up the phone call. He understood me just like Medium Bonnie had a long time ago. But I had still not officially been accepted into the program. I continued to wait and wait once again. Weeks went by and I realized that I had never had so much trouble giving anyone my money before, but it showed me that he wouldn't work with just anyone. It takes much more than money to be trained by Medium Joe. I admired that about him and decided I would accept my fate either way.

Then one morning, I opened my email and saw the subject line "Congratulations Raymond! You have been accepted to the two-year mentoring program." I was elated, and I can promise all of you there will be a second book. A book that will pick up where this one leaves off. A new chapter of my life and my development. I look forward to sharing it with you.

CHAPTER 37:

To Share and to Show

Do you remember Jessica's and my breakthroughs in Hot Springs with Medium Bonnie? This was the story about the retreat in the dome. Jessica and I had to find our purpose of being in this life. Mine was **"to share"** and Jessica's was **"to show."**

The entire purpose of writing this book was for me **"to share"** with you the fact that our lives never end; **"to share"** with you that we transform just like all energy transforms from one type to another, and another, and yet another; and **"to share"** with you we are all collectively part of one universal energy. You may call it God, the Universe, or the Divine. Call it what you will, but we are all one, and as one, we will transform and live on, far beyond this world that we know of now into a truly amazing place that very often visits us in the here and now.

This is the beauty of my discovery. Take these words with you and live. When the end of this life is near, there is nothing to fear. It is simply a transformation of your energy-based consciousness evolving into a newly formed energy-based entity that is part of all things. All things of this Earth and well beyond Earth, into a cosmic universal consciousness that surrounds us and connects everyone.

Take comfort in the fact that there is more after death. Live with that comfort in your mind. Live each day as though it were your last. And most importantly, go out **"to share"** this information with the ones you love. If you need help sharing or simply don't know how, Jessica is here **"to show"** you how.

I thank you for taking the time to read my book. There are millions of books you could have read, but you chose mine, and for that, I am eternally grateful. Perhaps there was a reason you chose this book. Remember, there really are no coincidences.

The light within me honors the light within you.

The End

Made in the USA
Middletown, DE
09 September 2021